BrightRED Study Guide

Curriculum for Excellence

N5

ENGLISH

Dr Christopher Nicol

BrightRED
PUBLISHING

First published in 2013 by:
Bright Red Publishing Ltd
1 Torphichen Street
Edinburgh
EH3 8HX

Reprinted 2013, 2014 and 2016. New edition published 2018

A CIP record for this book is available from the British Library

ISBN 978-1-84948-329-2

With thanks to:
PDQ Digital Media Solutions Ltd (layout), Ivor Normand and Elizabeth Fletcher (copy-edit and proof-read)

Cover design and series book design by Caleb Rutherford – e i d e t i c

Acknowledgements
Every effort has been made to seek all copyright holders. If any have been overlooked, then Bright Red Publishing will be delighted to make the necessary arrangements.

Brian A Jackson/Shutterstock.com (p6); NADIIA IEROKHINA/Shutterstock.com (p7); An extract from the article 'Red hair is a beacon in a sea of mediocrity', by Rosemary Goring, taken from 'The Herald', Monday 2nd July 2012 © Herald & Times Group (pp9–10); bzuko22 (p9); bzuko22 (p9); Claudia Meyer (p9); Jeka/Shutterstock.com (p10); len-k-a (p10); funkyfrogstock/Shutterstock.com (p10); len-k-a (p11); Vanessa Zanini Fernandes (p11); Brendan Howard/Shutterstock.com (p11); An extract from 'Michael Morpurgo interview' by Hermione Hoby, from 'The Daily Telegraph' 30 May 2011 © Telegraph Media Group Limited 2011 (p12); Tim Duncan/Creative Commons (CC BY 3.0)[2] (p13); Neil Williamson/Creative Commons (CC BY-SA 2.0)[3] (p14); Wanchai Orsuk/Shutterstock.com (p16); An extract from the article 'How to survive in the age of distraction' by Johann Hari, taken from 'The Independent' June 24th 2011 © The Independent (p18); An extract from the article 'The Passion of the Morrissey' by Chloe Veltman taken from 'The Believer' July-August 2012 Music Issue © Chloe Veltman (p18); An extract from the article 'Cycling Scotland's new Hebridean Trail' by Jonathan Thompson, taken from 'The Guardian' 01 September 2012. Copyright Guardian News & Media Ltd 2012 (p19); Hans Gruber/Shutterstock.com (p20); An extract from 'Why you can never look good in a fur coat' by Hadley Freeman, taken from 'The Guardian' 07 February 2011. Copyright Guardian News & Media Ltd 2012 (p20); Elnur/Shutterstock.com (p20); Ronan Crowley/Creative Commons (CC BY-ND 2.0)[1] (p21); An extract from the article 'Paradise Found' by Paddy Woodworth, taken from 'The Irish Times', September 1st, 2012 © Paddy Woodworth (p21); wavebreakmedia/Shutterstock.com (p23); magicinfoto/Shutterstock.com (p24); Monkey Business Images/Shutterstock.com (p26); Daniel_Dash/Shutterstock.com (p27); Joyce Vincent/Shutterstock.com (p28); Pavel L Photo and Video/ Shutterstock.com (p31); Sanja Gjenero (p33); Image taken from 'The Strange Case of Dr Jekyll and Mr Hyde: A Graphic Novel' by Robert Louis Stevenson (Author), Alan Grant (Editor), Cam Kennedy (Illustrator), published by Waverley Books Ltd; First edition (21 Feb 2008) © DC Thomson books (p34); ronstik/Shutterstock.com (p36); Chris Dorney/123rf (p38); Andy Dean Photography/Shutterstock.com (p39); RTimages/Shutterstock.com (p41); Davide Guglielmo (p42); bzuko22 (p63); bzuko22 (p43); Extracts from 'The Strange Case of Dr Jekyll and Mr Hyde: A Graphic Novel' by Robert Louis Stevenson (Author), adapted by Alan Grant, Cam Kennedy (Illustrator) Waverley Books Ltd; First edition (21 Feb 2008) © DC Thomson books (pp44–5); Photo © Independent Talent Group Ltd (p55); Image licensed by Ingram Images (p57); A photo from the Matrix Theatre Company production of Bold Girls taken from http://www.matrixtheatre.com/shows/boldgirls.html © Matrix Theatre Company (p59); An extract from 'Bold Girls' copyright © 1991 Rona Munro (pp61); Photograph by Eileen Heraghty/7:84. Reprinted by permission of the Trustees of the National Library of Scotland (p63); Photo © Canongate Books (p64); An extract from the short story 'Hieroglyphics' by Anne Donovan and the book cover of 'Hieroglyphics And Other Stories' © Canongate Books Ltd. reproduced with permission of Canongate Books Ltd. (p68); Photo © Claudia Kraszkiewicz (p72); The poem 'Siesta of a Hungarian Snake' by Edwin Morgan from 'Collected Poems' (Carcanet Press, 1990), copyright © Edwin Morgan 1990 (p72); Extracts from 'In the Snack-bar' by Edwin Morgan. Taken from Collected Poems (Carcanet Press, 1990), copyright © Edwin Morgan 1990 (p73); NonSense/Shutterstock (p74); The poem 'Tithonus' by Alfred Tennyson, 1833 (public domain) (p74); The poem 'Glasgow Sonnet No 1' by Edwin Morgan. Taken from Collected Poems (Carcanet Press, 1990), copyright © Edwin Morgan 1990 (p76); Ashley Van Haeften/Creative Commons (CC BY 2.0)[4] (p77); National Printing & Engraving Company, Chicago/ Creative Commons (CC BY-SA 3.0)[2] (p81); Lucky Business/Shutterstock.com (p86); eelnosiva/Shutterstock.com (p89); dotshock/Shutterstock.com (p91); Aniblo (p91); Leroy Skalstad (p91); Sanja Gjenero (p91); An extract from 'A Chitterin Bite' by Anne Donovan, taken from 'Hieroglyphics And Other Stories'. Published by Canongate Books 2004. Reproduced by permission of Canongate Books Ltd. (p92–3); Stefan Wagner, trumpkin.de (p92); Zurijeta/Shutterstock.com (p93); An extract from 'Black & Blue' by Ian Rankin, published by Orion Books Ltd 1997 (p94); An extract from 'The Cutting Room' by Louise Welsh, published by Canongate Books Ltd 2002 (p94); Korionov/Shutterstock.com (p95); Iancu Cristian/Shutterstock.com (p96); maga/Shutterstock.com (p97); Andi Collington (p98); Iablonskyi Mykola/Shutterstock.com (p99); Ned Horton (http://www.HortonGroup.com) (p99); Jelle Boontje (p99); Emilian Robert Vicol/Creative Commons (CC BY 2.0)[4] (p101); Calin Tatu/Shutterstock.com (p102); Wallenrock/Shutterstock.com (p105); Cartoon by Mac [Stan McMurtry]: 'Good news, George. Apparently our gas bills might be a few pence cheaper'. Originally published in: Daily Mail 14/12/2012 © Associated Newspapers Limited (p107); Giuseppe_RShutterstock.com (p108); Seth Sawyers/Creative Commons (CC BY 2.0)[4] (p122); bzuko22 (p123); bzuko22 (p123).

[1](CC BY-ND 2.0) http://creativecommons.org/licenses/by-nd/2.0/
[2](CC BY 3.0) http://creativecommons.org/licenses/by/3.0/
[3](CC BY-SA 2.0) http://creativecommons.org/licenses/by-sa/2.0/
[4](CC BY 2.0) http://creativecommons.org/licenses/by/2.0/

Printed and bound in the UK, by Charlesworth Press.

CONTENTS

INTRODUCING NATIONAL 5 ENGLISH

Welcome to the new and revised version of our National 5 Study Guide. Over the years, it has been responsible for helping countless students achieve exam success. Now, in its updated format, it is even more in tune with students' hopes and examiners' expectations.

There's quite a lot to come to terms with in this course, but broken down as it will be here, the structure is fairly straightforward. So, what actually is the course structure?

THE EXTERNAL ASSESSMENT

At the course's end, you will be assessed externally by two components:

Component 1 – The Exam

This is made up of a question paper in which:

- 30 marks will be allocated to a RUAE exercise on a non-fiction text

- 20 marks will be allocated to the production of a critical essay on a text which you will have studied in class

- 20 marks will be allocated to answering questions on a short extract from a Scottish fiction text which you will have studied in class, and you will also be asked to relate aspects of the extract to ideas and/or **themes** that you have noticed elsewhere in the work(s) you have studied.

Component 2 – The Portfolio

This is a portfolio incorporating two pieces of writing in different **genres**: one broadly creative, the other broadly discursive. 15 marks will be awarded for each of these.

In total, Component 1 accounts for 70% of the total mark and Component 2 accounts for 30%. Your final grade will be determined by your performance in these two components.

THE CHALLENGES AHEAD

Preparation for the course will involve you in refining a variety of skills in several areas. Let's take a quick look at the work involved in them:

Reading for Understanding, Analysis and Evaluation

The questions you will encounter here will be based on a non-fiction text of roughly 1000 words, usually taken from a quality non-fiction text. Your final score will be determined by:

- how well you *understand* what is going on in this text

- your ability to *analyse* how the writer makes his/her effects

- your ability to *evaluate* how well you feel these effects are made.

Critical Essay

It is one thing to read and enjoy a play, novel, short story or series of poems in class, and quite another to write about all this in an essay which does full justice to your understanding and enjoyment of the text. How to go about reading and interpreting the questions, how to structure your introduction, body paragraphs and conclusions, how to plan and deal with quotations: all these are set out carefully to optimise success under exam conditions.

contd

Scottish Context Exercise

Here, many of the skills you have been learning in preparing for your Critical Essay and Reading for Understanding, Analysis and Evaluation will serve you well again. **Metaphors**, **similes**, **alliteration**, **onomatopoeia**, **themes**, the effects of **imagery** and **word choice** on readers: all these and more will be needed to ensure you can answer detailed questions on selected passages from the Scottish texts(s) you have been studying in class. There will be the added challenge of relating this passage to other works by the same author or other sections of the work in question.

The Portfolio

Here you have a variety of choices to make. We will help you decide what your strengths and weaknesses are. Are you most comfortable with personal or reflective writing? Or does your enjoyment lie in creative writing? Perhaps you like researching key current topics and examining their pros and cons in a balanced analytical way? Or maybe you enjoy getting up on your soapbox and arguing for and against an issue, using all the persuasive techniques you have learned here? The ways and means to any of these responses are clearly laid out for study in the Portfolio section.

So there you have it. National 5 broken up into its constituent parts. And to deal with their various challenges, you will have our help at every turn. In addition, we will also be providing you with tips and suggestions for remembering key points in our 'Don't Forget' and 'Things to Do and Think About' text boxes. There will also be online activities to allow you to check on your progress as you go along. So how about getting down to familiarising yourself with the contents of this guide right now?

ONLINE

This book is supported by the BrightRED Digital Zone – log on at www.brightredbooks.net/N5English to unlock a world of tests, videos, games and more.

THINGS TO DO AND THINK ABOUT

If you are not already a regular reader of quality journalism, biography, travel writing and such texts, now might be a good time to start familiarising yourself with examples of these genres. The more familiar you are with the writing techniques employed by writers in such genres, the less daunting their challenges will be come the RUAE paper on exam day. Many quality newspapers will allow you to access their pages free online.

READING FOR UNDERSTANDING, ANALYSIS AND EVALUATION

AN OVERVIEW

The RUAE paper will represent 30 of the 70 marks of your final National 5 examination paper. As it forms such a significant proportion of your final grade, its challenges need to be fully met.

But what exactly will these challenges be? What kind of text, you may be asking yourself, will I be faced with? What type of questions will I be expected to answer? What kind of reading skills will it set out to test? What question-answering techniques will I be expected to know? How do I set about learning them?

These are just a few of the questions to which we will be helping you find answers in this section of this book. So, let's get started.

THE TEXT

The text on which you will be asked to answer a series of questions will be selected by the examiners from a non-fiction text of distinction. Quality journalism, biography and travel writing are the kinds of texts you can expect to encounter. So, it would be wise to make sure you are familiar with writing of these genres long before the exam. Whatever form the final choice takes, the text in question will run to around 1000 words and will foreground the types of writing skills and techniques on which you will be expected to comment fully.

ONLINE

To test your knowledge of RUAE questions and suitable answers, take the quiz at www.brightredbooks.net/N5English

THE QUESTIONS

You will be expected to answer questions which will test your ability to <u>understand</u>, <u>analyse</u> and <u>evaluate</u> the article's content in some detail. You will also be asked to give broader answers which will test your ability to <u>infer</u> the author's general intentions in certain areas of the text and to <u>summarise some key ideas</u>. The number of marks allocated to each question will be clearly marked, thus helping you to manage your time appropriately. Let's take a brief overview of what your responses need to cover in each of these categories.

Understanding questions

These are by far the most straightforward questions to answer. They mean just what they say: they test your grasp of *what* the piece is all about and probe your understanding of certain items of vocabulary; you may also be asked to suggest *why* certain comments are made. Being able to paraphrase ideas and expressions from the text is of prime importance here.

DON'T FORGET

Horses for courses. If a question is only worth 2 marks, don't waste 10 lines answering it; conversely, if it's worth 4 marks, a single line simply will not do.

contd

You will also need to be able to summarise key information from an indicated stretch of text, using bullet points if you wish. There will also be questions testing your ability to infer what the writer is hinting at but not saying outright – in other words, 'reading between the lines'. When you are tested on your understanding, you will be expected to answer in your own words.

Analysis questions

These are a bit more demanding. Here you need to look at *how* a writer created a certain effect, by identifying how certain techniques and words or phrases are used to create that effect. Here you will need to quote certain items from the text, identify the technique at work and suggest what its effect on the reader is. The skill here is knowing the various techniques at work and being able to comment on them.

Evaluation questions

These ask you for your opinion of *how well* you think something has been said. To do this, you will need to find items of evidence to back up your assessment: a particularly successful simile, for instance, or a striking contrast in the choice of words which will form the basis of your comment. You may well have commented on these already in an Analysis question, but now you need to develop your own 'take' on them.

These three categories of question become much more manageable if you think of them simply under the following two headings. Look out for certain key words indicating to which category the question belongs. We will start to look at these key words in the next chapter.

Questions broadly about understanding	Questions broadly about analysis
• Questions which test factual information i.e. *understanding* • Questions which ask you find to find key points i.e. *summarising* • Questions which ask you to work out what the writer is suggesting without saying directly i.e. *inferring*	• Questions which test your knowledge of language features and how they work on the reader. i.e. *analysing* • Questions which ask you to say how well in your opinion certain features work i.e. *evaluating*

DON'T FORGET

Questions broadly about analysis will always need quoted items from the text as evidence for your answer. Questions broadly about understanding put the emphasis on using your own words.

ONLINE

Regular reading of quality newspapers such as the *Scotsman*, the *Herald*, the *Guardian*, the *Independent* and so on will do much to boost your performance not only in RUAE work but also in discursive Portfolio work. Remember that many of the quality journals will also let you read them online. Try, for example, clicking the link to the '*Scotsman*' at www.brightredbooks.net/N5English, and then tap on the *Scotsman* strapline at the top of the page. Scroll down to 'Opinion' and 'Comment' pieces which deal with issues of the day. These are the basis of many a RUAE article.

THINGS TO DO AND THINK ABOUT

You will have read enough by now to know that the key to a successful RUAE score is to *read quality non-fiction on a regular basis*. It might be a newspaper, it might be a biography, it might be travel writing, but make a point of making contact regularly with this kind of writing from today. Don't leave it until nearer the exam. The wider your reading, and the more extensive your vocabulary, the greater your chances of success.

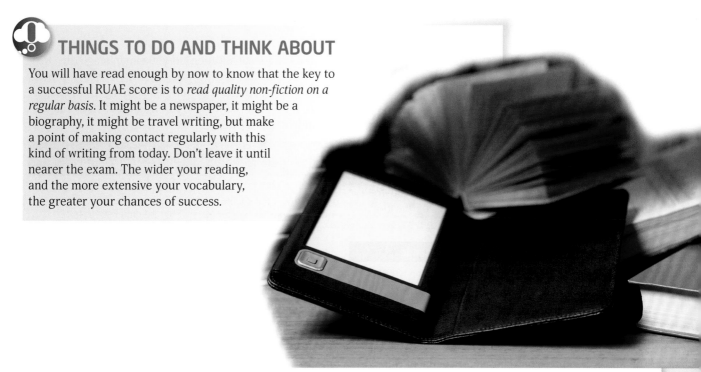

UNDERSTANDING

RECOGNISING THE QUESTIONS

The wording of questions testing understanding may take a variety of forms, but here are some possible formats:

Explain in your own words what the writer feels about...

Explain what is meant by the expression...

As far as possible in your own words, _summarise..._

Explain in your own words why this advice might be seen as...

Why does the writer say about...

Questions of this kind are testing:

- your basic understanding of the text
- your ability to express this understanding _in your own words._

ONLINE TEST

To check your knowledge of understanding questions, visit www.brightredbooks. net/N5English

 **ACTIVITY**

Which of these questions are testing understanding? Why have you rejected the other questions? What do your rejected questions seem to be asking you to do?

• Show fully how the writer's word choice or sentence structure in lines 15–19 helps convey his ideas effectively.	• Explain in your own words two aspects of 'pleasure' or 'happiness' as defined in the past and two as defined today.
• Explain what the attitude of the judge is to this type of driving.	• Pick an expression from the final paragraph (lines 88–94), and show how it helps to contribute an effective ending to the passage.
• Explain in your own words what the writer means when he calls continuous assessment a 'valid alternative'.	• Show fully how the writer conveys his friend's apparent attitude, and his actual attitude to his decision.

DON'T FORGET

Avoid repeating any word or part of the word in the expression you are being asked to explain. Be sure to cover all the words in an expression, not just the most obvious one.

EXPLAINING IN YOUR OWN WORDS: WHAT DO I CHANGE?

As we said above, you are being tested on your understanding of the factual content of certain passages, but you are also being tested on your ability to express this information in your own words, without 'lifting' words or expressions from the passage. But the examiners are reasonable people; there are certain items you are allowed to retain in answering these types of questions, certain you need to change. So, what are they?

Items to keep	Items to change
Proper nouns Common nouns with no obvious alternatives: _crocodile, brakes, mortgage etc._	Verbs, adverbs, adjectives and figures of speech will all need to be rephrased in your own words.

Beware 'word-for-word' substitutions

The words or expressions chosen for comment will require some careful thinking to ensure you have covered ALL elements in them. Avoid struggling for word-for-word substitutions. If you can manage this, well done. But most of us may have difficulty coming up with precise 'translations'. A better idea is to try to explain, or gloss, the idea rather than try to find exact substitutes for individual words.

Possible question	Possible answer explaining the underlying idea
Explain in your own words what the writer means when he describes the waiter as 'grudgingly polite'.	The waiter was showing good manners/ being courteous but he didn't seem to be doing this very willingly/ enthusiastically.

Tracking down the answer

In Understanding questions, a good tip is to adopt a two-stage approach:

Stage 1: Highlight or underline the words or phrases in the text where you know the answers lie.

Stage 2: Work now on putting these words or phrases in a new way, perhaps reshaping the section entirely to make it your own.

THINGS TO DO AND THINK ABOUT

Let's try that out:

> Since the day the Romans stepped beyond Hadrian's Wall, enemy armies have probably come to a halt at the sight of the Scottish infantry: short, red-headed blokes who might at first look like stunted carrots, but turn out to be ferociously terrier-like. Their latter-day equivalents were the likes of Jimmy Johnstone and Billy Bremner, dinky-sized footballers who ran rings around their opponents, and in so doing gave their fellow gingers a much-needed confidence boost.

'Red hair is a beacon in a sea of mediocrity', Rosemary Goring, *Herald*, 2 July 2012

Using your own words, explain why over the centuries it has been a mistake to judge Scottish soldiers and footballers by their appearance.   2

So, what are we to highlight? 'Over the centuries' suggests that we are looking for one reason from the distant past and maybe also a later one. (There are also two marks at stake, so two examples might be a good idea.) So, what surprised the Roman soldiers? Maybe the fact that these short men, who looked like 'stunted carrots', turned out 'to be ferociously terrier-like'? And, more recently, there were 'dinky-sized' footballers 'who ran rings round their opponents'? So, we are looking for our own way of constructing an answer from these highlighted items which together say *outwardly unusual (short, red-haired) – yet surprisingly effective, not just then but later, too.* So, how about this?

'ferociously terrier-like'	*In Roman times, the odd appearance of short, red-haired Scottish troops may have failed to impress the invaders who, nevertheless, found them to be fierce and determined fighters. Similarly, it was a mistake more recently to look down on certain short, red-haired footballers since they far outperformed rival players.*	'stunted carrots'
'ran rings round'		'dinky-sized' 'fellow gingers'

What about these answers?

With a partner – or as a class – look at these answers and say what kind of mark you would give them. Explain in detail your reasons for awarding your mark.

Although their appearance was against them, Scottish soldiers in Roman times were good fighters. More recently there have been good, short footballers.

Short, red-haired Scotsmen have always been good in battle and in sport.

In Roman times red-haired Scottish soldiers frightened the invaders and so have some red-haired footballers more recently.

Despite looking unusual, being short and red-haired, the Scottish soldiers never gave up on their fierce attacks on the Roman invaders. In later years, some Scottish footballers of similar appearance were equally effective when confronting the opposition.

DON'T FORGET

To explain in your own words you need a good vocabulary. That is where regular wide-reading of quality newspapers and literature will help you. A good vocabulary is built up over time. You can't acquire one the night before the exam!

UNDERSTANDING: PRACTISING QUESTIONS

Here are some more questions on extracts from Rosemary Goring's article 'Red hair is a beacon in a sea of mediocrity', featured in the *Herald*, 2 July 2012:

1 When you think of how many talented redheads we've had, from Mary, Queen of Scots to Ewan McGregor, it's anyone's guess where the stigma comes from. Some, apparently, used to think it was a sign of immorality, as if devilish flames were licking around the person's head. Personally, I love it: whether it's a Tilda Swinton burnt orange, or a Robert Redford strawberry blonde, all reds are beautiful. Sadly, though, not everyone would agree. And perhaps because women have been more easily able to disguise their natural shade, it's men who continue to bear the brunt of an entrenched prejudice which, under the term 'gingerism', is deemed by some to be as serious a form of discrimination as racism.

(a) Using your own words, give two reasons why the writer believes criticism of redheads is unjustified.   2

(b) What is the meaning of 'stigma'? How did the context help you work this out?   2

(c) What does the expression 'entrenched prejudice' suggest about the public's view of male redheads?   2

(d) Explain in your own words what the writer means by 'gingerism'.   2

2 So, even though chemists' shelves abound in russet hair-dyes, the fear of red lives on. Admittedly there was a flurry of interest in redheaded men when the American thriller *Homeland* was aired this spring with Damien Lewis in the main role. A glance at Lewis's career, however, shows that he's made a living playing sinister characters, as if his coppery thatch was a convenient shorthand for viewers. Benedict Cumberbatch, meanwhile, toned himself down to a dull brown to play Sherlock Holmes, and Michael C. Hall, from *Dexter* and *Six Feet Under*, is boringly mousy in both series when in reality he could effortlessly hide himself in a field of pumpkins.

(a) Using your own words, explain why the writer believes 'the fear of red lives on'.   2

(b) Explain in your own words why a 'coppery thatch was a convenient shorthand for viewers' in the selection of Damien Lewis for this particular role.   2

3

I simply don't understand why anyone would camouflage themselves as brunette or black or even blonde when they could stand out like a lighted match, a flaring beacon in a sea of mediocrity. I just hope Merida's crimson curls mean redheads finally get the respect they deserve. Otherwise, they will surely soon be dyed out of existence.

(a) What does the expression 'a flaring beacon in a sea of mediocrity' suggest about the writer's view of red-haired people?   2

(b) In your own words, suggest what the writer means by claiming that redheads will 'soon be dyed out of existence'.   1

Check your answers with a partner, and get a third person to comment on how fully each of you has fulfilled the demands of the question, avoiding as far as possible any use of words from the original text. Only then look up the suggestions for answers on our Digital Zone.

ONLINE TEST
For more practice at understanding questions, test yourself online at www.brightredbooks.net/N5English

ONLINE
For suggested answers head to www.brightredbooks.net/N5English

DON'T FORGET
There is more than one way of expressing an answer to any of these questions.

DON'T FORGET
Understanding questions do not just test your comprehension of information; they also put your vocabulary under the spotlight. You must not fudge this with 'lifts' from the writer's text. Are you working on developing vocabulary by regular reading of quality journalism? If not, it's time you started!

THINGS TO DO AND THINK ABOUT

Comment with a partner on the following answers to question 1 (a) above. You need to consider not just the accuracy or otherwise of the comment, but also to what extent the students have used their own words. How many marks out of two would you award each one?

1. Since we've had many talented redheads from Mary Queen of Scots to Ewan McGregor, it's anyone's guess why they are disliked. She also thinks they are all beautiful.

2. She believes that over the centuries there have been many able, clever redheads, which make this criticism unjustified. She also feels that people with red hair are most attractive.

3. She does not know where the stigma comes from, and in her opinion it is not a sign of immorality as was once thought.

4. Mary Queen of Scots and Ewan McGregor show that having red hair shows talent, and in addition she finds them to be very attractive.

UNDERSTANDING: SUMMARISING

Once again, we come upon a question type which tests your vocabulary and ability to pinpoint key information concisely.

'Lifting' words and expressions in questions is to be avoided. Additionally, you will need to take stretches of the text in question and reduce it to its essential message, cutting out interesting but non-essential detail. That's the real challenge, perhaps: making up your mind what to remove. Then, in your own words, you have to summarise as briefly as possible what remains.

LET'S TRY THAT OUT

The challenge lies in finding your own words to express the writer's ideas – but this time as economically as possible. Let's try working an example together.

So what do I leave out?

In summarising, it is of prime importance to eliminate any details, no matter how interesting, which obscure the main points being sought. Usually, you can present these in bullet point form or in very brief sentences. And, of course, in your own words as far as possible.

- figures of speech e.g. similes, metaphors
- examples
- lists
- comparisons
- descriptions

DON'T FORGET

Learning to summarise effectively is essential for performing successfully in the N5 English exam. Summarising, however, is a life skill which will prove useful well beyond N5 English. At college, university or in a commercial workplace, you will find the ability to reduce complex information to its essentials a skill you will need time and again. Master it now.

ONLINE

Read the full interview, 'Hay Festival 2011: Michael Morpurgo interview' online at www.brightredbooks.net/N5English

ONLINE TEST

For more practice on summarising questions, test yourself online at www.brightredbooks.net/N5English

EXAMPLE:

Here is an interview with writer Michael Morpurgo, author of more than 100 books for young people, discussing the need to talk to children about the world as it is, no matter how grisly.

> Morpurgo is adamant about darkness being a necessary component of children's literature. 'Our great problem', he explains, 'is that children now know whatever they want to know – at the press of a button they can discover all horrors of the adult world.'
>
> He adds: 'They know very early on that the world is sometimes a very dark, difficult and complex place, and the literature they read must reflect that. Otherwise we're just entertaining them to pass the time. And what's the point? Let them watch television if that's all there is to literature.'

('Hay Festival 2011: Michael Morpurgo interview', Hermione Hoby, *Daily Telegraph*, 30 May 2011)

In your own words, explain fully why Morpurgo sees that it is 'necessary' for children's literature to tackle 'darkness'.

4

First, we need to decide what the key ideas are. But we can't just 'lift' them; we need to paraphrase them into our own words. We also need to reduce them to their essentials. And, in a summary, we have no room for phrases like 'at the press of a button' or 'a dark, difficult and complex place'. These are too detailed, as well as not being our own!

Let's take it a step at a time: what are the key ideas of the first section? And can we eventually paraphrase them into our own expressions in brief bullet points, rather than take just individual words? Let's see.

How about saying 'Morpurgo insists that ...'?

Morpurgo ... adamant ... darkness ... necessary component ... children's literature

How about saying 'Through television ...'?

Problem ... at the touch of a button ... discover ... all horrors of the adult world

contd

That would seem to give us two bullet points:

- Morpurgo insists that evil must be included in children's novels.

- Through television, they quickly discover the many nastinesses of grown-up life.

Now, using the same technique, see what you get with the second part of the extract.

- What they read has to engage with these problems.

- If it doesn't do so, it is no more serious than television.

EXAMPLE:

Now try this example of summarising on your own. If you get stuck, you will find a suggested answer on the BrightRED Digital Zone. It describes how Scottish novelist Ian Rankin's *Black & Blue* marked a change in the author's approach to fiction writing.

> *'Black & Blue' marked more than a commercial breakthrough, however, for many of the novels which followed manifested not only a newly found density and complexity of plot-lines but a keener awareness of contemporary social issues. Admittedly, this had been present before in Rankin's output, as for example, in 'Mortal Causes' (1994) where sectarianism and paramilitary activities were important elements in the plot but in 'Black & Blue' the moral and social issues connected with the de-commissioning of North Sea oil-platforms may be seen to be becoming more all-embracing of the novel's life.*

In your own words, explain fully how *Black & Blue* was a 'breakthrough' in Rankin's fiction.

4

ONLINE

Head to www.brightredbooks.net/N5English to see a couple of suggested answers for this question.

THINGS TO DO AND THINK ABOUT

In summarising, avoid <u>figurative language</u> of all kinds: metaphors, similes and so on. Avoid also <u>examples</u>, <u>lists</u>, <u>comparisons</u> and any <u>details of secondary importance</u>. As in understanding questions, concentrate on using your own words and on <u>reducing ideas to their essentials</u>, not just reducing the number of individual words. Try to vary your sentence structure from that of the original; it will lead you away from being tempted to use features from the original too closely.

Remember, your summary can be conveyed in bullet points.

DON'T FORGET

The wider your vocabulary, the easier you'll find it to summarise in your own words. So, if you're not already doing so, get reading quality texts of all kinds!

UNDERSTANDING: INFERENCE

These are broader understanding questions which are asking you to look below the surface of the text. You are being asked to 'read between the lines', so to speak, and make some deductions of your own about:

- what the writer is hinting at
- what he/she is feeling

You are being given clues, but the writer's intention is not being fully spelt out. You need to be sensitive to the 'vibes' coming off the text to understand the writer's full intentions. Picking up these 'vibes' accurately will boost your mark usefully.

HOW DO I WORK THIS OUT?

From accumulated information

Sometimes, there will be an accumulation of factual information.

EXAMPLE:

> *A year-long feast of colour and scents, the Angus Glens offer motorists, hill walkers and cyclists an accessible opportunity to explore the Scottish landscape at its best. The scents of moorlands and grasses, the cries of the curlew, the chatter of rocky burns are all to be found in this sometimes overlooked corner of Scotland.*

Referring to the information offered here, explain fully in your own words how the writer makes clear his view that the Angus Glens are an ideal holiday destination.

3

ANSWER:

So, let's work out an answer for this question. Remember, there are three marks on offer which suggests our answer might benefit from pointing to three items of information. And we are required to answer in our own words. So, what items might we pick out to suggest an 'ideal holiday destination'?

Selected information	Own words
'year-long feast of colour and scents'	Ideal since attractive at any time
'accessible' 'motorists, hill walkers, cyclists'	Ideal since easy for all to get there
'landscape at its best'	Ideal opportunity to view unrivalled natural scenery

Putting all this information together, we might get this possible answer for three marks:

By indicating that the Angus Glens can be visited at any time, are easy to get to and offer tourists some of Scotland's finest scenery, the writer makes clear he views the Angus Glens as an ideal holiday destination.

(An alternative item might have been 'sometimes overlooked', suggesting the glens may not be too crowded.)

ONLINE

For more on inference, check out: 'BBC Bitesize: Inference Questions' at www.brightredbooks.net/N5English

contd

From explaining features of language

Sometimes, you may be asked to look at certain features of language such as word choice, imagery or sentence structure to identify how the writer suggests an attitude, feeling or reaction.

EXAMPLE:

Read this description of winter before looking at the following question.

> *If the sun was sluggish and ineffective no such fault could be found with the winds that screamed over the moors and in the chimneys of farm and cottage, for they were as strong wild horses, and biting as fine hail. Woe to the ears that were exposed to the full force of the blast on the uplands for that were seared as with hot irons.*

(Adapted from W. Riley, *Men of Mawm*)

With reference to two examples of the writer's language show fully how he makes clear the violent nature of the winter weather.　　4

ANSWER:

As before, we need to find features of language, suggesting this time the violence of the weather over the moors. Here, the most obvious features are three similes and an item of word choice:

Selected feature of language	Your possible comment
'Screamed'	The word choice here suggests the wind sounded as if it were alive and crying out violently.
'as strong as wild horses'	The wind seemed to have the amazing strength of an untamed animal.
'biting as fine hail'	The wind was so sharp it seemed to pierce your skin like hail.
'with hot irons'	It left anyone exposed to it feeling as if they had been the victim of instruments of torture.

Piecing this together, we might start to write our answer, remembering that the question requires 'two examples of the writer's language' for our four marks. So, we might offer one example of word choice and a simile:

'Screamed': the writer's word choice suggests the wind seemed personified, crying out violently.

'As with hot irons': the simile suggests the wind was so strong it seemed to be burning your ears like an instrument of torture.

THINGS TO DO AND THINK ABOUT

Inference questions build on the understanding and analysis skills you are acquiring elsewhere in your RUAE preparation. Examine examples of any interesting word choice or figurative language you notice. Be on the look-out, too, for words with thought-provoking connotations. Work out for yourself why these particular features of language have been selected. Think about what the writer might be hinting at through their selection.

DON'T FORGET

Inference questions require just as much skill in using your own words as more straightforward understanding questions. Once again, a good grasp of **synonyms** is useful.

DON'T FORGET

Always check the marks on offer. A question offering three marks requires either more explanation or more examples than one giving only two.

ONLINE TEST

For more practice at inference questions, test yourself online at www.brightredbooks.net/N5English

ONLINE

How did you get on? Visit www.brightredbooks.net/N5English for a suggested answer.

ANALYSIS

RECOGNISING THE QUESTIONS

Analysis questions are sometimes thought to be a little trickier to answer than understanding ones. They are there to test your ability to analyse *how* writers make their effects on readers. These questions demand a little more from you and may carry more than two marks to reflect this.

Normally you will need to do three things:

1 <u>Locate</u> relevant words or phrases from the text for your answer – again, highlighting these is a good idea.

2 <u>Identify</u> aspects of **style** at work: for example, simile, inverted sentence structure, list and so on.

3 <u>Explain</u> in your own words the <u>effect</u> this item is having on readers.

The analysis questions can often be identified by their frequent use of the word <u>how</u>:

Comment on <u>how</u> the writer's use of imagery shows ...

<u>How</u> does the writer convey his fear of ...?

Suggest <u>how</u> the writer shows her disapproval of ...

But, be careful! The analysis question may be expressed in other ways:

Explain fully the appropriateness of the word ...

Quote an expression from the first sentence which ...

Comment on the effectiveness of the sentence structure ...

Identify and briefly explain the writer's use of ...

These are just some of the ways you will be expected to show your analytical skills in exploring the text in question.

LITERAL LANGUAGE VERSUS FIGURATIVE LANGUAGE

Before we go any further in tackling analysis questions, it will help if we sort out the distinction between **literal** language and **figurative language**.

In understanding questions, we are often being asked about the literal meaning of statements made or information given in the text:

> *What reasons does the writer give for ...?*
>
> *Explain why the writer dislikes ...*
>
> *Explain what the writer means by 'silent witness' in the first sentence.*

In other words, the questions are testing our powers of understanding words in their everyday or dictionary meaning. If, for instance, we say:

> *Our fields were in great need of water, and many communities went hungry*

we are talking in literal language. But if we say:

> *Our fields were crying out for water, and famine stalked the land*

we have changed from literal to figurative language.

Put simply, figurative language puts 'figures' (or pictures or images) into our text which help to convey the meaning much more vividly and dramatically than literal language. Not only has information about

contd

shortage of water and risk of starvation been conveyed, but also it has been conveyed in a way which creates illustrations in our imaginations. For here the fields are presented almost as people, shouting out to demand water, while famine, like some evil threatening giant, prowls around the communities.

Figurative language not only conveys meaning; it also pictures meaning. And, as the saying goes, a picture is worth a thousand words. Now let's explore some examples available to writers in this world of **imagery**.

IMAGERY AND OTHER LITERARY DEVICES

DON'T FORGET

Your knowledge of figurative language needs to be really thorough – not just for your **RUAE** work but also for writing **Critical Essays** and **Scottish Context** work.

Some analysis questions may test your knowledge of the various techniques that writers employ to create the images in figurative language. You are expected to comment on these. So, you need to locate what you see as an appropriate illustration of this technique ('*the buzzing of bees*', '*like a thief in the night*'), identify it (*alliteration, simile*) and then explain what effect this choice by the writer is having on the reader. Before going further, you need to be sure of what figurative language techniques are available to authors. Let's look at them.

The English language is rich in figurative language devices, and a full list of some of the most common can be found in the Glossary at the end of this book. There are some, however, which tend to be found frequently in exams of this kind.

These devices fall broadly into two categories: those which conjure up visual pictures, and those which create pictures in sound – aural pictures, you might say.

Visual imagery	Aural devices
Simile: a comparison between two items using 'like' or 'as'. *He's like a dog with a bone.* The effect of similes and metaphors is to add pictorial emphasis/impact to the written description.	**Alliteration**: the repetition of a particular consonant – or consonant sound – at the beginning of a group of words to create a certain sound effect. *Cold clay clads his coffin.* Here the harsh sound of the letter 'c' matches the grimness of the description. *Soft sighing of the southern seas.* Here the soft 's' sounds mimics the gentleness of the water's sound.
Metaphor: also a comparison, but this time the two items being compared are not 'like' each other, since one item becomes the other. *You're an angel.*	**Assonance**: the repetition of a certain group of similar-sounding vowels in words close to each other, again used to create a certain aural effect. *And murmuring of innumerable bees.*
Personification: yet another way of making a comparison. Similes and metaphors can become examples of personification when an inanimate object (without life) is spoken of as if it were human and alive. *The wind howled down the corridor.*	**Onomatopoeia**: here the sound of the word mimics its meaning. *Clink, fizz, rip, honk, boom, purr* suggest their meaning in their sound.
Hyperbole: an exaggerated image to create a certain effect (often humorous) or to emphasise something. *The list goes on for miles. He never fails to get lost.*	**Enjambment**: in poetry, this is the running-on of one line into another or into several others, often to give either a conversational feel to the content or sometimes to suggest speeding up for an effect of urgency. It can also make the reader wait for a key point to be made when the sentence finally stops. *... for my purpose holds To sail beyond the sunset, and the baths Of all the western stars, until I die.*

THINGS TO DO AND THINK ABOUT

Each of the following phrases is an example of one of the visual or aural imagery techniques described above. Match each example to its literary device:

She's as light as a feather.

The moonbeams kiss the sea.

He's a millstone round her neck.

Your bag weighs a ton.

Splash!

Crumbling thunder of seas.

Peter Piper picked a peck of pickled peppers.

Alliteration

Onomatopoeia

Personification

Hyperbole

Assonance

Metaphor

Simile

ONLINE

Now that you know something about the differences between figurative and literal language, you might like to try recognising some figurative items on your own. Before we start practising exam questions, why not ease yourself into the recognition process with a game of Hangman? Try 'Figures of speech' found at www.brightredbooks.net/N5English. Work on your own or with a partner.

ANALYSIS: IMAGERY

WORKING WITH IMAGERY

It's one thing to know the more common items of figurative language, quite another to be able to recognise them at work and to comment on the effect they create.

SOME PRACTICE QUESTIONS

Here are some questions which use the visual-imagery techniques from the table on the previous page. Work through these examples on your own, using the table to help you before looking at suggested answers on the Digital Zone. We'll be working on the examples in the right-hand column later.

ONLINE

For suggested answers to each of these practice questions, head to www.brightredbooks.net/N5English

Johann Hari reflects on a science-fiction novel he has been reading about an imagined world where books have been forgotten:

I have been thinking about this because I recently moved flat, which for me meant boxing and heaving several Everests of books, accumulated obsessively since I was a kid. Ask me to throw away a book, and I begin shaking and insist that I just couldn't bear to part company with it, no matter how unlikely it is I will ever read (say) a 1,000-page biography of little-known Portuguese dictator Antonio Salazar. As I stacked my books high, and watched my friends get buried in landslides of novels, it struck me that this scene might be incomprehensible a generation from now. The book – the physical paper book – is being circled by a shoal of sharks, with sales down 9 percent this year alone. It's being chewed by the e-book. It's being gored by the death of the bookshop and the library.

(Adapted from Johann Hari, 'How to survive in the age of distraction', *Independent*, 24 June 2011)

(a) Show how the writer's imagery makes clear the number of books he possesses. **2**

(b) How does the writer use imagery to make clear the threat to the paper book? **2**

Chloe Veltman writes about the reaction of the audience to the stage performance of the British singer, Morrissey:

The gladioli are in flight. On the stage of the Henry Fonda Theatre in Hollywood, a slender man in heavy 1950s style eye-glasses, floral shirt, white jeans and pompadour hairdo is energetically hurling a bunch of gangly blooms into the audience whilst singing something about spending warm summer days indoors writing frightening verse to a buck-toothed girl in Luxembourg. In the auditorium, tough-looking twenty-somethings in cuffed jeans, baseball boots and voluminous quiffs sing word-perfectly along, their eyes shining as they strain to catch the somersaulting stems like blushing bridesmaids outside a country church. Gradually, the adoration turns into unabashed devotion, as people try to clamber onto the stage. Those that make it past the heavy-set bouncers cling desperately onto their pop idol like lepers begging for a miracle.

(Chloe Veltman, 'The passion of the Morrissey', *The Believer*, July–August 2012 Music Issue)

(a) How does the writer use imagery to suggest that the 'tough-looking twenty-somethings' are not as tough as they appear? **2**

(b) Identify and explain the imagery by which Veltman makes clear the strength of the fans' 'devotion'. **2**

contd

Jonathan Thompson takes off on a cycling holiday in the Outer Hebrides but runs into difficulties finding a taxi to get him from the airport to his hotel:

'Don't worry,' says the lady who makes the tea in the arrivals/departures/ baggage lounge. 'The Post Office van will take you.' Half an hour later, I'm helping the local post lady, Morag, with her round – bouncing alongside her in the battered red van like a cross between Marty McFly and Jess the Cat. As we drive across the loch-dotted landscape, locals get into and out of the back of the van like human parcels, delivering themselves en route. They chat to each other in Gaelic, with a few English words – 'carpet' … 'loony' … '90-odd quid' – popping up like remote Atlantic islands.

(Adapted from 'Cycling Scotland's new Hebridean trail', *Guardian*, 31 August 2012)

(a) Comment on how the writer uses imagery to show that he does not take his situation too seriously. **2**

(b) Using your own words, explain fully how the writer continues the idea that passengers were 'like human parcels'. **2**

(c) Identify the means by which the writer develops the idea that English is not greatly used by the island's Gaelic-speakers. **2**

ONLINE TEST

For further revision of the use of imagery, test yourself online at www. brightredbooks.net/N5English

THINGS TO DO AND THINK ABOUT

In all of your answers, you will have had to locate the image itself, identify the figurative device in question (simile, metaphor etc.) and then – most importantly of all – look for what links the two things being compared (e.g. a comparison between Mount Everest and a pile of books suggests that the pile of books reaches vast heights, just as Everest does). Once you have done this, you need to explain the effect the image has on you, the reader. So, we might have something like this as an answer to that first question:

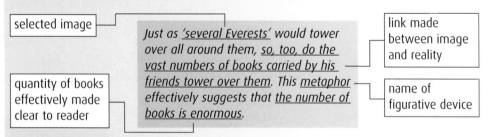

selected image

quantity of books effectively made clear to reader

Just as 'several Everests' would tower over all around them, so, too, do the vast numbers of books carried by his friends tower over them. This metaphor effectively suggests that the number of books is enormous.

link made between image and reality

name of figurative device

Consider your answers to the previous questions again. Have you fully located, identified and explained the effect of the imagery in each?

ANALYSIS: WORD CHOICE

WORKING WITH WORD CHOICE

Like imagery, word choice deals in pictures, too. But this time, the picture is created not in the writer's head but in yours, the reader's.

In other words, word-choice questions exploit the associations which we make with certain words. Often, we do not consciously think about these associations. Word-choice questions, however, will make you do just that. We call these associations in our heads **connotations**.

EXPLORING CONNOTATIONS

Think about the dictionary definition (or **denotation**, if you wish) of *thin*. A dictionary definition might be *having little flesh on the body*. The following words could in certain circumstances be used as possible alternatives, but which of these would you like to be called? What are the connotations of each one? Discuss with a partner or in a group what kind of thinness is suggested by the picture conjured up by each word. Attractive? Unattractive?

scrawny slender lean cadaverous skinny spare underweight svelte slight slim

Verbs, too, can paint pictures, just like adjectives. Consider for a moment the neutral statement:

> *Blair walked into the room.*

'Walked' is a neutral word, free of any connotations. But were we to replace 'walked' with any of the following, what would the connotations tell us about the mood, feelings or appearance of Blair?

slouched strode crept skipped waddled

Discuss with a partner or in a group what you feel the connotations to be.

LET'S TRY THAT OUT

Hadley Freeman is appalled by the fact that the wearing of real fur might be making a comeback.

While fur is obviously disgusting, it is also incredibly useful in that it alerts you to the fact that the person wearing it is a complete moron, without you having to waste time talking to them.

('Why you can never look good in a fur coat', Hadley Freeman, *Guardian*, 6 February 2011)

(a) Show how the writer's word choice alerts you to her contempt for the wearers of fur.   2

To answer a word-choice question, you need to be on the lookout for words or short expressions that leap out at you as suggesting a colourful attitude to something under discussion. The words chosen will be far from neutral in their effect on readers. So, here we might end up with three possible candidates:

'disgusting' suggests that she looks down on the wearer with scorn.

'(complete) moron' suggests that the wearer is seen as a total idiot by the writer.

'waste (time)' suggests that discussion with the wearer is wholly pointless.

Answering tip: word-choice questions can be answered very directly: select a word, place it in inverted commas and follow it with *suggests/gives the impression that/makes me think of* – then, in your own words, state the associations (or connotations) you have with it.

20

If you think there might be two words making up a phrase, put the less essential one in brackets.

You do not need to write in full sentences. Avoid phrases longer than two or three words; examiners would then ask which word it is you have actually chosen.

Paddy Woodworth returns to Vietnam to evaluate the developing tourism product that is Phu Quoc.

It's still quite easy to walk alone on an idyllic beach in Phu Quoc, and imagine you are the only person on a pristine island. It's even easier to imagine you are alone if you walk 100 metres into one of the remaining patches of majestic jungle.

But it is not as easy as it was. We first went to this Vietnamese treasure in the Gulf of Thailand five years ago. Already the high-rise hotels on some stretches of the west coast were reminiscent of the worst of the Costa del Sol, with outraged TripAdvisor reviews to match.

This time around, we could see from the plane that many hectares of jungle had been gouged out for a massive international airport in the middle of the island. Unless a few resorts that offer tourists real encounters with Phu Quoc's remarkable environment and culture can turn the tide, the fate of yet another 'paradise island' seems sealed.

In reality, of course, neither the beaches nor the jungle have been truly pristine for a very long time. They have been fished and logged for many centuries, but only recently, and quite abruptly, has their exploitation threatened to become unsustainable. And Phu Quoc has probably never been much of a paradise for its own people, and certainly not over the last century.

During the worst years of the American war (as they understandably remember it here), the South Vietnamese army, allied to the US, established a huge prison camp on the island for NLF insurgents. After the latter's victory in 1975, the new communist authorities turned it into a rather grim museum, billed as one of the top 10 tourist attractions today.

Phu Quoc also saw fierce fighting between the new government and the notorious Khmer Rouge, who claimed it for Cambodia, in the early 1970s. Today the island is at peace, though the rush to development makes life a grim struggle for the poor. The small capital, Duong Dong, boasts markets that offer dazzling cornucopias of local produce: fish, fruit, spices and vegetables of mind-boggling diversity and often – to us at least – startling shapes and colours. The prices also seem rock-bottom to our pockets, but many local people can't afford them.

Wander just 50 metres off the tourist trail, and you will encounter hovels that match anywhere in Asia for abject poverty, in sharp contrast to the often garish McMansions that are springing up along the main roads.

(Paddy Woodworth, 'Paradise found', *Irish Times*, 1 September 2012)

(a) Show how the writer's word choice in the first two paragraphs helps us to understand his admiration for the beauties of the island.

2

(b) Show how the word choice in paragraphs three and four expresses the writer's distaste for what is happening to the island.

2

(c) How does the writer use word choice in the last two paragraphs to contrast the attractions and horrors of the island?

2

Here you need to be confident in expressing what image you take away from the writer's selection of vocabulary: for example, *'garish McMansions' makes me think of hideous, brightly coloured buildings that are as alike as any McDonald's hamburgers.*

 ONLINE TEST

For more study on how to spot and answer word-choice questions, visit www.brightredbooks.net/N5English

 THINGS TO DO AND THINK ABOUT

We all carry connotations of words in our heads; it's just a question of digging deep and articulating the image that comes to mind.

ANALYSIS: PUNCTUATION

WORKING WITH PUNCTUATION AND SENTENCE STRUCTURE

So far in our survey of analysis questions, we have been commenting on how writers make *expression* more vivid within a sentence.

Now we turn to looking at the sentence itself and the features that help shape it: punctuation.

A basic understanding of the contribution of basic punctuation marks to a sentence is essential. The good news is that they are easily mastered. You need to be familiar with the following punctuation marks and, as with other types of analysis questions, be prepared to discuss the <u>effect</u> of their use on the sentence.

Full stop	.	Its position indicates the completion of a sentence. The position of the full stop in a paragraph determines whether we are dealing with long or short sentences. The effect of each we will discuss shortly.
Comma	,	Usually used to separate brief items in a list. *Apples, pears, bananas and a grapefruit.* Used before and after a phrase, commas are said to be used as **parenthesis** markers. *Enter Arthur, a distant cousin, in love with Anne.* The phrase *a distant cousin* is said to be <u>in parenthesis</u>. When answering questions, we say 'The phrase in parenthesis adds additional information about …' See also pairs of dashes and brackets below.
Semi-colon	;	Often used to separate larger items in a list. *A beach house in Bermuda; a flat in Paris, on the Champs Elysées no less; a chalet in the Alps; a castle in Scotland with over 40 rooms: all these were owned by their aunt.* They also indicate a turning point in a balanced sentence. *Sober, he was unpredictable; drunk, he was dangerous. To err is human; to forgive divine.*
Colon	:	A colon may signal an explanation or elaboration that is to follow. *It was now night: stars twinkled overhead and the moon was rising.* Or it may signal an upcoming quotation. *Criticised for being harsh, Les replies: 'Heart like a flint, that's me.'* It may also introduce a list. *Her garden was a picture: marigolds, lupins, roses, daisies and, in spring, masses of tulips.*
Dashes and brackets	– – ( )	Pairs of dashes, brackets or commas on either side of a phrase – *her mother's cousin* – are used to create what we call a phrase <u>in parenthesis</u>. When answering questions, we say 'The phrase in parenthesis adds additional information about …' An individual dash can be used to add emphasis or importance to a word or phrase following it. *And there it lay before them, glittering in the blue Aegean – Hydra.* An individual dash can sometimes also be used as a kind of informal colon, indicating a concluding list or explanation. *He had taken great trouble over their evening meal – prawns, roast venison and a fine raspberry tart.*
Ellipsis	…	In mid-sentence, these three dots can be used to suggest an interruption, hesitation or indecision. Used at the end of the sentence, they can suggest anticipation or suspense. *The door opened and a hand appeared …*
Exclamation mark	!	Usually used to indicate strong emotion on the part of the writer: often surprise, excitement or anger. *It was Bill!*

contd

ONLINE TEST

To see how well you know your punctuation, test yourself at www. brightredbooks.net/N5English

DON'T FORGET

If a question asks you to comment on sentence structure, the first thing to do is check out the sentence to see if any of the above punctuation marks could be the basis of your answer. It might be as simple as that. But make sure you say what the effect of the punctuation is.

Question mark	**?**	To indicate a question, which may be a structuring device for that section of the article – i.e. the writer asks a question and then proceeds to answer it in the following paragraph. A series of questions may well be there to signal the writer's confusion or bewilderment. *Who could she turn to? Was there anyone she could trust? What if they were all against her?* Sometimes this can mark the end of a **rhetorical question**, which invites readers to share the writer's views. *What kind of society turns its back on those in need?* You need to say precisely what the apparent aim of the writer is: for example, 'to win the reader's support <u>for his views on what constitutes a just society</u>'.
Inverted commas (quotation marks)	**' '**	Around an individual word or phrase, inverted commas suggest that the writer is casting doubt on the surface meaning of the word. *I had little faith in the 'help' being offered by the bank.* Here the writer is indicating that the 'help' is so-called help, rather than real assistance. Quotation marks are also used to indicate the title of a poem, a song, an article or a chapter in a book. (The title of a book, a film or a play is indicated in print by italics, but in handwriting you would use underlining or perhaps quotation marks.)

THINGS TO DO AND THINK ABOUT

If a question invites you to comment on the writer's language, as it often will do, you can point to all sorts of things: imagery, sentence structure, **tone** or word choice – but don't overlook punctuation. By all means, talk about these other aspects; but, if you are stuck for a comment, examine the passage's punctuation and its effect on shaping the writer's meaning. This could be the means of picking up a valuable mark or two.

ANALYSIS: SENTENCE STRUCTURE

Now, while a good writer can make a sentence do almost anything, the sentences on whose structure you will be asked to comment tend to fall into certain recurring categories. Again, it is the *effect* of these sentence-structure choices which the writer has made that you will be asked to comment on.

WORKING WITH SENTENCE STRUCTURE

You have just learned all about different types of punctuation that you are likely to encounter in your RUAE work. The chances are, however, that you will need to discuss punctuation in combination with some of the sentence features discussed below. So, what might you expect to be asked about? Here are some strong possibilities.

Long sentences	Used to suggest the sheer length of something, a route of a river or road, for example, or the complexity of a process, or the boredom of something dragging on and on.
Short sentences	Used to intensify the impact/drama of what is being said. A brief remark in a sentence of its own gains greatly in dramatic effect.
	And with that, she left.
	Any form of persuasive writing, such as advertising, may well make use of the short sentence.
	Try it. You'll love it. Everyone does.
	Be very alert to the power of the short sentence after a particularly long one: the dramatic impact is increased even more.
A list (neutral, with climax or anti-climax)	Used to underline/emphasise/highlight the sheer number of items, actions or people being described.
	Always check lists out for additional possibilities. It might build to a **climax** –
	She had played hostess to generals, princes, kings and even the mighty Napoleon himself.
	– a technique which adds to the impact of the final item.
	It might, however, end in an **anti-climax** –
	His case contained a pair of Gucci loafers, a Rolex watch, cologne by Chanel and a pair of dirty underpants.
	– a technique which is usually used for humorous effect.
	Of course, it might simply be a neutral list! But it's a sound idea to check out any list for climax or anti-climax.
Sentences without verbs	These are known as minor sentences. Sometimes they create a chatty, informal effect.
	Great! Another fine mess. What next?
	Or they can function like the short sentences described above: to add dramatic impact.
	A woman's glove. Slightly blood-stained.

contd

Inverted word order	Normal word order in English tends to follow this pattern: *He was fierce in his claim to innocence.* But, to emphasise/underline/highlight a certain element in the sentence, we can invert the normal order, usually to place the important word(s) first. So, we get *Fierce he was in his claim to innocence.* But the inversion can also be manipulated to place the important word to be emphasised at the end, thus giving *In his claim to innocence he was fierce.* Exam tip: if you cannot see anything at all in a sentence to comment on, check out inversion. It is often one of the last things we think of. And it *might* just be the right answer!
Repetition	This may take the form of repeated words or phrases to underline/intensify the idea the writer is seeking to emphasise at a particular point. *A good cyclist needs ... A good cyclist hopes that ... But a good cyclist knows above all that ...* Note that these repetitions in the closing stages of a text might be building to a climax. It is worth mentioning in your answer if you detect this.
Balanced sentences	When writers wish to make us strongly aware of some contrast that they want to indicate, they sometimes resort to these. They are recognisable by the semi-colon (;) that acts as a pivot, or balancing point, in the middle of the sentence. *Alive, she had been seen as a saint; dead, she was quickly demonised.*
Rhetorical question	These are questions expecting no direct answer, rather the reader's support for the writer's views. *Who wants to see a child suffer in this way?* Here the reader is expected to share the writer's horror at the ill-treatment of children.
Parallel structures	These are patterns of either phrases or words which give a pleasing predictability and **rhythm** to the sentence. The effect is to add emphasis to what is being said. *It is <u>by logic we prove</u>, but <u>by intuition we discover</u>* (da Vinci). *The ants were everywhere:* climbing *over jampots,* swarming *under the sink,* scrambling *into cupboards,* diving *into the bin.* The likeness of pattern here (verb + preposition + noun) makes for a more memorable phrase and creates a greater impact than a less patterned structure would.

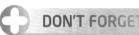

DON'T FORGET

You need to know by heart these forms of sentence types, and the punctuation listed earlier, so that, when faced with sentence-structure questions, you run through them all in your mental checklist of possibilities without wasting precious time.

THINGS TO DO AND THINK ABOUT

Find and read an article from the Comment section of a respected newspaper, either in print or online, and analyse the punctuation and sentence structure used throughout the piece. Remember to use the highlighting technique mentioned earlier in this chapter. Did you notice any of the techniques mentioned above being used? To what effect?

ONLINE TEST

To see how well you know your sentence structure, test yourself at www.brightredbooks.net/N5English

ANALYSIS: PUNCTUATION AND SENTENCE STRUCTURE COMBINED

When faced with a question about sentence structure, remember that it is extremely difficult to draw a hard line between sentence structure and punctuation. You should be alert to the fact that mention of a feature of one might lead you into a discussion of the other. This can only enrich your answer. And remember, there is a limited number of possibilities in answers of this type; so make sure you know all of them well in advance of the exam.

DON'T FORGET

As with other analysis questions, questions asking you to look at sentence structure or punctuation will expect you to say what effect a particular sentence feature has on the reader. That does not mean generalising; it means spelling out how that particular feature works in that particular sentence. So, an answer might look like this: *The writer uses* **parallel structures** *to say the ants were everywhere: 'climbing over jam pots, swarming under the sink, scrambling into cupboards, diving into the bin'. The likeness of pattern here (verb + preposition) creates the idea that the ants were busy getting absolutely everywhere, completely invading the kitchen.* Don't just quote your notes and say 'The parallel structures create a memorable phrase and a greater impact than a less patterned structure would'. You <u>must</u> relate the feature to the actual **context** in front of you.

LET'S TRY THAT OUT – 'A TIME BEST FORGOTTEN'

It might have been decades ago, but I remember the anguish of that first day as if it were yesterday. I remember the howling when my mum left me with Mrs Bell. I remember the strange looks the other kids gave me when I was at last coaxed into the classroom. Other people remember, too, and any time I meet up with them, they never let me forget this.

I remember it all: the seemingly vast building, the coal-fired stove, the 'large' pupils in primary 2, the honky-tonk tinkling of the piano, the endless school day, walking home in the winter dark. A time best forgotten.

(a) Show how the writer's sentence structure in paragraph one emphasises the point being made about unhappy experiences.   **2**

(b) Show how the writer uses sentence structure in paragraph two to draw attention to the power of memory.   **2**

(c) How does the writer use sentence structure in paragraph two to underline the unhappiness of that early time?   **2**

(d) Explain how the writer's language shows that his memory of the Primary 2 pupils might not have been quite accurate.   **2**

LET'S TRY THAT OUT – 'THE PERILS OF OPTIMISM'

The fitness culture is everywhere. Think about how often we run into sweaty bodies in lycra – some decidedly unappealing in this most unforgiving of materials – when trying to negotiate our way home from work. Think of the number of times fit young men and women look out at us from media advertising exhorting us to buy such and such a health-giving product. Think of the times we look sadly at our expanding waistlines and begin to wonder if perhaps it is not too late to do something about it. In pessimistic moods, such reflections are depressing; in optimistic moods, they're downright dangerous.

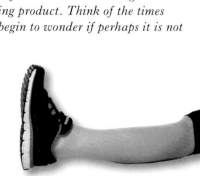

(a) Suggest two ways in which the writer here uses sentence structure to underline the points he is making about what he sees as our obsession with fitness. **4**

(b) What purpose do the dashes serve in sentence two? **2**

Appearing in court to give evidence, Cluny seemed to Usher to be a very different man from the sad man he'd seen two weeks before in his office: alert, youthful-looking, enjoying himself mightily. From the dock, Anderson looked on sneeringly, as if Cluny's treachery was just another harsh lesson in the wicked ways of fate in his life. And life is what he got.

(a) Show how the writer uses sentence structure to emphasise how appearing in court had changed Cluny. **2**

(b) How does the writer's sentence structure bring out the severity of the sentence? **2**

Fiona had never cared for the Festival: traffic, never exactly free-flowing, came to an almost dead stop; tourists seemed to clog up all the pavements; her friends took off for all points of the compass; she could never get into her favourite restaurants; the infernal din of the Tattoo kept her awake for hours; there was always the feeling that she was about to have her pockets picked; and this morning there was a dead man in her front garden.

'I'm not sure how to say this,' she explained to the police when her shock allowed her to get to the phone, 'but when I went out this morning, there was … I found … well, he was … dead.'

(a) Show how the writer's sentence structure adds impact in paragraph one. **3**

(b) How does the writer use sentence structure to convey the girl's state of mind in paragraph two? **2**

 ONLINE TEST

For more practice at identifying sentence structure and punctuation use, test yourself at www.brightredbooks.net/N5English

 THINGS TO DO AND THINK ABOUT

What have we learned here? Firstly, you really have to know the function of the various punctuation marks and the possible choices available to writers when considering sentence structure. Secondly, you will not impress examiners if you simply identify the writer's selected feature(s). You must say what its *effect* is on the reader.

ANALYSIS: TONE

WORKING WITH QUESTIONS ABOUT TONE

Our ears are quick to detect tone in conversation. We can hear quite well when people are being, say, chatty or humorous or persuasive or emotive or ironic or matter-of-fact. Facial expressions and body language help spell this out. But trying to pin down the tone in a written piece of text can be more tricky. One writer has called tone 'the unspoken attitude of the author to his subject and/or audience'. We need to look for clues or markers in the text which help us to make out what this 'unspoken attitude' might be.

Writers can create tone by a whole variety of means, but here are some clues to determining tone.

Tone	Markers	Intended effect
Chatty/informal/colloquial	• Short sentences • Abbreviations: *can't, it'll, won't* • Free use of first/second-person pronouns: *I, you* • Chatty expressions: *Come on! Right on! No problem.* • Free use of exclamation and question marks • Sentences without a verb (minor sentences): *No change there then.* • Slang expressions: *Back in a jiffy, a smack on the gob.* • Informal commands: *Go early/Take a picnic/Stay away from...*	To get persuasively closer to the reader, giving the effect of someone chatting informally to his/her friends.
Humorous	• Use of exaggeration or a series of exaggerations (also called hyperbole): *He was so thin I've seen more fat on a chip!* • Telling jokes/stories against the speaker or topic • Mixing formal and informal styles: *Please refrain from asking for credit as a smack on the gob frequently offends.*	To strive for comic effect, sometimes simply to amuse, but sometimes to underline and mock the absurd/pointless nature of some issue under discussion.

contd

developments (scene by scene, act by act) another to themes. In this way, you can slip in new information as your study progresses. Novels and poems could be organised along similar lines. By exam revision time, you will have a powerful means of bringing together all your acquired knowledge on a text in one place. This approach can easily be adapted to a pc filing system, if you prefer working on computers. (But be sure to back everything up!)

Your essays and discussions: when you get an essay back from your teacher, read the comments carefully and store the essay in your text-specific file. You will have spent some time on the essay, so don't let this valuable revision aid go to waste. Think, too, of various discussions you may have had in class. You will remember good points better if you make notes at the time.

Published commentaries: these can be helpful, but they are no substitute for the notes you have made in class. These commercial notes may take a different approach from your teacher and you may become confused between the two sources of information. Avoid at all costs 'lifting' from these study notes without acknowledging where these comments came from. Remember, the markers will probably be familiar with these commentaries, too!

SELECTING AN EXAM QUESTION

Time is precious in the exam. You need to select a question promptly, but certainly not casually. Hence the need to know your texts really thoroughly. Because if you know your texts in depth, you are better placed to make a rapid mental survey of them to decide which question your knowledge best equips you to answer.

The selection process

Once you have decided you have sufficient information to settle on a question, begin by reading the question carefully. Underline or highlight what you think are key words.

> **EXAMPLE:**
>
> For instance, you may select a question like this:
>
> **Choose a short story or novel in which setting figures prominently.**
>
> **Describe the contribution of the setting and then show how this feature helped your understanding of the text as a whole.**
>
> Underline the words that are pointing you to what the essay will be about. In this case, the words will probably be *setting figures prominently.* In the second line, you will also probably have underlined *Describe the contribution.* Notice, however, that there is a second part to the question:
>
> **... and then show how this feature helped your understanding of the text as a whole.**
>
> In exam questions at this level you must always be ready for this second part. Under all the pressure to write down all the details of setting which you wish to 'describe', you must not underestimate the importance of 'how this feature helped your understanding of the text as a whole'. For this is the key part of the question; by keeping it constantly at the forefront of your mind as you write, you are creating the clear line of thought which will shape your essay – and win the marker's approval. Referring back to this second part in each paragraph will help you stay on task.

ONLINE TEST

For more practice on reading the question, test yourself online at www. brightredbooks.net/N5English

DON'T FORGET

You need to convince the examiner in the structure of your essay that you can do here exactly what you do in Paper 1:
· *understand* the writer's intentions
· *analyse* how he/she creates effects
· *evaluate* what is being achieved.

THINGS TO DO AND THINK ABOUT

Consider the following question:
Choose a poem which arouses strong emotion in you.
Describe how you feel about the poem, and explain how the poet leads you to feel this way.
How do the words in the question help you to understand how you should answer? What two things does the question ask you to do? Highlight the parts of this question that would shape your essay.

PLANNING A RESPONSE

A plan is necessary for two people: you and the examiner. Start writing without a plan, and you risk going off task and not answering the question. Consequently, you sell yourself short and do not make the most of your text knowledge. Similarly, the examiner fails to see your line of thought in answering the question – and marks you down.

For practice, let's return to our focus question on page 33 and apply it overleaf to a short novel for which it would work well: Robert Louis Stevenson's *The Strange Case of Dr Jekyll and Mr Hyde*.

PRE-PLAN BRAINSTORMING

Before we plan, let's take a look at that rapid mental survey we need to make before beginning to write. We need to consider

- how well a question matches up to our knowledge of this text. (Do I know enough about 'setting' to answer this one?),

- the *precise* demands of our selected question, and

- what our line of thought in answering it might be.

We're not quite at a plan yet, just a speedy mental process – but a vital one before we get to a plan. It might go a little like this:

What we know about setting	What line of thought might be
Sordid and attractive houses in same street	*Stevenson believes man has two sides to nature*
Jekyll's handsome house linked to broken down laboratory	*Same split exists all around us, not just in human nature*
Several key events happen at night.	*Split not always visible*
Do I have evidence to illustrate all this?	*Setting helps lays this out physically for reader*
	Jekyll maybe not unique.

A POSSIBLE APPROACH TO PLANNING

Everyone has his/her way of planning an essay. Some make lists of points they wish to include, linking them to particular characters, settings or themes.

Others may prefer diagrams or a mind-map of the kind here. Here is how our earlier brainstorming might work out as we get down to assembling more detailed material:

ONLINE TEST

For more practice on planning a response, test yourself online at www.brightredbooks.net/N5English

Point 1:
Sordid and attractive mixed up in opening description

… the street shone out in contrast to its dingy neighbours, like a fire in a forest.

… freshly painted shutters, well-polished brasses, and general cleanliness and gaiety of note …

BUT … *a certain sinister block of building thrust forward its gable on the street.*

… and bore in every feature the marks of prolonged and sordid negligence.

The door […] was blistered and distained. Tramps slouched in the recess …

Point 2:
Direct linking of Dr Jekyll's handsome home to this sordid building

Round the corner from the by street there was a square of ancient, handsome houses, now for the most part decayed from their high estate.

One house wore a great air of wealth and comfort.

Question: why does Stevenson link them? Making a point about duality? Respectable Jekyll's connection to the sordid?

Choose a short story or novel in which setting figures prominently.

Describe the contribution of the setting and then show how this feature helped your understanding of the text as a whole.

 DON'T FORGET

A list of your statements will keep you on task. It will also help you to judge your time appropriately. Don't get bogged down in any single one.

Point 3:
Several key events take place at night/in fog

I was coming home from some place at the end of the world, about three o'clock of a black winter morning … (Hyde's attack on child)

Utterson first encounters Hyde at night

Danvers Carew is murdered at night

Jekyll's death/final transformation into Hyde takes place at night.

A great-coloured pall lowered over heaven …

… the fog settled down again upon that part, as brown as umber and cut him off from his blackguardly surroundings.

Question: why darkness and fog? Night mirrors darkness of J's intentions? Fog aids concealment, used literally and metaphorically?

 DON'T FORGET

A good statement sets out the agenda for the section you are about to embark on. It also announces the general area for discussion. Save the back-up evidence (detailed textual reference and quotations) for the upcoming analysis. If you get into detail too quickly, what are you going to discuss later?

THINGS TO DO AND THINK ABOUT

After setting out in your plan all the material you are going to use, start to group it into various headings or areas. Then create statements which sum up what you want to say about each heading/area. List them one under the other. Do they make a coherent line of argument? If they do, you have a miniature version of the essay you are about to write – and your essay is well begun.

STRUCTURING YOUR ESSAY

We have worked on a rough, overall plan for our essay on *The Strange Case of Dr Jekyll and Mr Hyde*. Now we need to transform it, step by step, into a full essay.

INTRODUCTIONS

Done clearly and concisely, your introduction will make a favourable impression on the marker.

You do not have much time to create this impression, so:

1   In your first sentence, make clear the title of the selected text (in inverted commas) and its author. (Nothing makes a worse impression than getting the spelling of the author's name wrong. Make sure checking basics like this is part of your revision process.)

2   In that same sentence, adopt some wording which suggests that you have chosen this text because it fits the set question.

Going back to the wording of the question on our Stevenson text, we might write as an opening sentence:

A novel in which <u>setting figures prominently</u> is 'The Strange Case of Dr Jekyll and Mr Hyde' by Robert Louis Stevenson.

3   The significance/role of setting in this essay briefly outlined. (It gives the marker a hint as to the direction of your line of thought.)

Respectable Dr Jekyll, impatient with the restraints of respectability, longs to indulge in hidden, evil desires. To do so, he invents a potion which turns him into wicked Mr Hyde, thereby living out his dark side in another self. In Jekyll, the virtuous and the evil live side by side, just as in the novel's setting the attractive and the ugly co-exist in the world around him.

4   Now revisit the wording of the second part of the question to assure the examiner you have not forgotten about that second part.

By frequently drawing attention frequently to the physical setting, and setting several key events at night, Stevenson uses these features of setting to help us understand what he is saying about the complex nature of man in the text as a whole.

Note that, in this example, we are giving not just a reference *back* to the question but also a reference *forward* to our 'road-plan' for the essay: discussion of the physical setting to be followed by discussion of the impact of night-time settings.

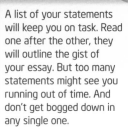

DON'T FORGET

A list of your statements will keep you on task. Read one after the other, they will outline the gist of your essay. But too many statements might see you running out of time. And don't get bogged down in any single one.

DON'T FORGET

Don't be scared to open a statement section with a question, particularly if it is reminding the examiner that you are respecting the wording of the question. *So, what are we to make of Stevenson insisting on placing the sordid next to the respectable? Well, it suggests ...*

ONLINE

To find out more about Robert Louis Stevenson and *The Strange Case of Dr Jekyll and Mr Hyde*, go to the Robert Louis Stevenson website at www.brightredbooks.net/N5English

ONLINE TEST

For more practice structuring your paragraphs, test yourself online at www.brightredbooks.net/N5English

BODY PARAGRAPHS: OPENING STATEMENTS

Our mind-map gave us some rough key points. Now we need to fashion them into the kind of statements which will be effective lead-ins to each paragraph in our essay, statements which demonstrate to the marker where our line of thought is going – and which keep us on task. A good statement sets the agenda for the paragraph. From the points in our mind-map, we might end up with statements such as these:

Statement 1: *In the opening chapter of* The Strange Case of Dr Jekyll and Mr Hyde, *Stevenson goes to great trouble to establish that the area around Jekyll's laboratory home presents a setting which is a curious mixture of the prosperous and the dingy.*

Statement 2: *There is yet a further contrast of environments, for we later learn that this squalid laboratory is connected to a grand building in a nearby square.*

Statement 3: *The setting is enriched even more by having the key moments in the story take place at night.*

A checklist for statements

- A good statement sets out a focussed agenda for the paragraph which follows.

- Sometimes, this may be a single sentence, sometimes called a topic sentence. Sometimes it may require two or three sentences to make the paragraph's key point.

- A good statement will always be fairly general and should not get down to specific details or quotations. Save these for the evidence section which follows the statement.

THINGS TO DO AND THINK ABOUT

Choose any poem which you have read recently which features an unfortunate character.

By referring to appropriate techniques explain how the poet brings the character to life for you.

- Brainstorm details of the character, techniques employed to make him/her interesting and what your line of thought might be.

- Organise your thoughts into a mind map (two or three main points may be enough).

You may wish to develop your plan into an essay.

STRUCTURING YOUR ESSAY (CONTD)

BODY PARAGRAPHS: SUPPORTING EVIDENCE

We have now seen the kind of statements needed to set out a clear agenda for a convincing paragraph. These statements form the paragraph's backbone. Now we need to put flesh on the bones. In other words, we must now find <u>evidence</u> to support the statements made at the start of the paragraph.

Evidence can take two forms: direct quotations from the text or detailed references to information in the text. A good essay will use both.

To see evidence at work, let's go back to our essay on *The Strange Case of Dr Jekyll and Mr Hyde*. One of our statements told us:

Statement: *In the opening chapter, Stevenson goes to great trouble to establish that the area around Jekyll's laboratory presents a setting which is a curious mixture of the prosperous and the dingy.*

Now we need to offer evidence to support this claim of a mixture of appearances:

Our evidence to support that statement: We find the street 'shone out in contrast to its dingy neighbourhood, like a fire in a forest'. Stevenson also notes the buildings presented, 'freshly painted shutters, well-polished brasses, and general cleanliness'. But Jekyll's laboratory sticks out harshly in this attractive area. We are told that 'a certain sinister block of building thrust forward its gable on the street'. This block 'bore in every feature the marks of prolonged and sordid negligence' and its door was 'blistered and distained. Tramps slouched in the recess...'

So, yes, we can now say we have supplied detailed evidence from the text to support our statement that the area was mixture of shabby and smart.

Put another way, our statement has shown our understanding of the text; our evidence has shown our analysis of the means by which the author has created his effects. Now, to complete our paragraph, we need a brief commentary on our evidence to give our evaluation of why we think this is a significant point to be making about the setting.

BODY PARAGRAPHS: CLINCHING COMMENTARY

Let's take stock for a moment: your paragraph has provided a clear statement; it has also supported that statement with detailed textual evidence. But what exactly is the reader supposed to make of this evidence? In other words, it might be sensible to unpack this evidence a little to explain to the reader how it establishes the point(s) you made back in your statement. You need to <u>evaluate</u> its significance to round off your paragraph.

Candidates sometimes panic at this point. 'What exactly *do* I think about this? What *should* I be saying?' is a common complaint. At this point, there are certain 'lead-in' phrases which can help focus your thoughts:

From evidence such as this, we can see that ...

Clearly then, Stevenson is guiding us to think that ...

This suggests that ...

From this, we may understand that ...

Alert readers will note/ conclude that ...

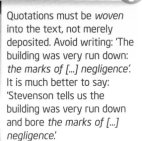

DON'T FORGET

Quotations must be *woven* into the text, not merely deposited. Avoid writing: 'The building was very run down: *the marks of [...] negligence'.* It is much better to say: 'Stevenson tells us the building was very run down and bore *the marks of [...] negligence'.*

ONLINE TEST

For more practice on introductions, test yourself online at www.brightredbooks.net/ N5English

contd

In essence, you are suggesting to readers what they are to make of all this. You are, in a sense, 'selling' your evidence to them. This is your opportunity to link the evidence to your line of thought which you set out away back in your introduction. So our paragraph might end along the lines of:

Clearly then, Stevenson is suggesting the area around Jekyll is a curious mixture of the smart and squalid. In other words, this is a neighbourhood whose identity is not clear-cut, one where the sordid cannot be separated from the attractive. <u>Given that Stevenson is suggesting elsewhere in the novel that man contains both the nasty and the virtuous within him, this split personality of the street helps us understand in a visual way that this split exists in society as well as in the individual. Stevenson seems to be hinting that Jekyll's divided personality may not be unique.</u>

And there you have it: a paragraph which shows understanding, analysis and evaluation. We might call it a SEC paragraph.

You have made a **statement** setting out a point about Jekyll's surroundings (showing *understanding* of the text).	S
You have produced **evidence** to support this point (showing *analysis* of the means whereby you came to this understanding).	E
You have helped the reader with an explanation of what all this evidence is suggesting by providing a **commentary** on it (showing an *evaluation* of the evidence's significance).	C

Using the SEC format will help you keep your paragraphs on track in a way that showcases your knowledge. It also helps the examiner see a clear pathway through your arguments.

 DON'T FORGET

Statement
SAY IT
Evidence
SHOW IT
Commentary
SELL IT

CONCLUSIONS

By the time you have covered your main points with SEC-type paragraphs, there isn't going to be much time left for a lengthy conclusion. If possible, try to round off your essay with a brief restatement of the main points that formed your line of thought throughout the essay. A good tip here is to have a number of synonyms up your sleeve so that your wording has some variety to it.

Make no new points here or seek to bring in quotations. You don't have time and they would only spoil the sharp focus of the rest of your essay.

If you have been referring to your line of thought in each paragraph, there is no need for an elaborate conclusion. Do not leave a great final statement of your line of thought to the conclusion: you might run out of time!

It is no bad idea to begin your brief conclusion with a phrase that signals the rounding off:

<u>Standing back from the text as a whole</u>, we see that Stevenson may be suggesting that ...

DON'T FORGET

If you have made your line of thought clear in every paragraph, your conclusion can be brief.

ONLINE

Read the handout 'Conclusions' for more on writing a good conclusion: www.brightredbooks.net/N5English. When you are struggling with what to write, play the 'So what?' game and refocus your mind.

 THINGS TO DO AND THINK ABOUT

The skills that helped you make sense of RUAE questions – the ability to understand, analyse and evaluate – are again proving useful in structuring persuasive critical essays. For the body paragraphs are structured around these same ideas, contained in the SEC format described above. It is the building block of the body paragraphs of critical essays. Use it.

MAINTAINING THE FLOW

The most successful critical essays follow a clear line of thought from start to finish. For this to be achieved, you cannot simply round up a few ideas, loosely related to the question, and call it an essay. There has to be a guiding idea or shaping principle, established in the introduction, which unites the ideas which you present in the various paragraphs. And these paragraphs, too, need to flow seamlessly, one to the next. Readers should not be pulled abruptly from one idea or one paragraph to the next and be expected to see a link between them somehow.

There are a number of signalling words, phrases and techniques which can help you to achieve this goal.

ONLINE

Discover some of the simpler signalling words by looking at 'Signal Words' at www.brightredbooks.net/ N5English. Many of these you already use to change direction, sequence events or illustrate your points. Familiarise yourself with the whole range available to you. Once you have done this, look at how the longer phrases we discuss below can also help you improve the flow of your writing.

FROM INTRODUCTION TO FIRST PARAGRAPH

A sensible idea in your introduction is to indicate in its last lines the areas you will be covering in your essay – creating a 'road-map', if you like. So, your introduction might end with the words:

Donovan arouses sympathy for the protagonist through her handling of Miss O'Halloran's social isolation, the use of **symbolism** *and the second-person narrative.*

Make sure you pick up your chosen topics *in the order mentioned* here, beginning the first SEC paragraph after the introduction with phrases such as:

Examining first Miss O'Halloran's social isolation, we notice that …

Isolated socially, Miss O'Halloran has only …

The social isolation of Miss O'Halloran is insisted on by Donovan throughout the short story.

DON'T FORGET

By spending time practising writing effective linking statements, you will dramatically improve your writing style and therefore your chance of success in the exam!

FROM ONE BODY PARAGRAPH TO THE NEXT

Once you have completed your discussion of your first point, your task is to ease the reader from this paragraph to your next point smoothly. In this example, you must lead the reader from your paragraph about Miss O'Halloran's 'social isolation' to your next paragraph, which should discuss the 'symbolism' in the story, the second area you mentioned in your road-map. This can be done effectively by using statements like these:

The sympathy aroused by the old lady's social isolation is further intensified by Donovan's use of symbolism.

Equally effective in arousing our sympathy for Miss O'Halloran is the way Donovan uses symbolism.

Symbolism is the second technique by which Donovan invokes our sympathy for her protagonist.

Note that all these sentences, as well as making good linking sentences, would also make useful opening statements which you could develop successfully to create a convincing SEC paragraph.

Successful flow is ensured by making a brief reference – direct or indirect – to the subject of your previous paragraph in the first sentence of your new one.

Once completed, this paragraph needs to be linked to the next one in the way you have done for this one. And so on.

DON'T FORGET

Note that all these sentences would make suitable statements which you could develop successfully to create a convincing SEC paragraph.

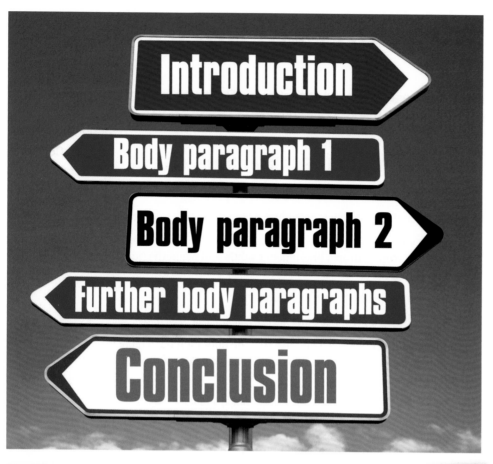

ONLINE

Read this *Guardian* article online: 'A sea of red that evokes thoughts of more than just algae' at www.brightredbooks.net/N5English – can you see how the first statement of each paragraph links to what has come before? This gives it a great flow and makes it easier to read. The same is true in your critical essay writing.

ONLINE TEST

For more practice on maintaining the flow, test yourself at www.brightredbooks.net/N5English

DON'T FORGET

If you take care with the smooth flow of one paragraph into the next, you will be helping keep your line of thought on track.

INDICATING A BRIEF CONCLUSION

Your essay's flow is neatly rounded off by signalling that the final stages are approaching with a 'summing-up' phrase, followed by a reminder of what was said in the introduction.

Seen overall, this is a short story in which the author successfully employs the techniques of ... to bring us close to the misery of ...

Standing back, we note that throughout the tale the techniques mentioned in the introduction have succeeded in ...

Summing up, we have seen the three techniques of ... have been successfully employed to arouse our sympathy for a character who ...

Not only is a conclusion indicated by an opening phrase of the type employed here, but also there is a reminder to the examiner of your loyalty to the points you raised in your introduction. In this way, your essay is rounded off briefly, but in a thoroughly satisfactory manner.

THINGS TO DO AND THINK ABOUT

Before testing out these suggested guidelines to improve the flow of your writing in a brand new essay, why not try this experiment? This you might do with a partner.

Take an essay which you have already written, and adapt the techniques and phrases we have been suggesting here to assist the smooth flow from one paragraph to the next. Do it in such a way that you lead smoothly from introduction to first paragraph, from paragraph to paragraph and then into the conclusion. You do not need to rewrite the whole essay, just the necessary linking sentences. Now read these links aloud to a partner. You will notice that you have added real authority to your writing. Try it.

PERFECTING YOUR PERFORMANCE

You are now in a position to create a successful critical essay. But there is always room to polish your performance to ensure optimum marks. Let's see how.

USING QUOTATIONS FOR MAXIMUM EFFECT

Longer quotations

There is more than one way to introduce a long quotation to your paragraph.

Sometimes you will pave the way for a quotation by first describing it. In this case, you should use a colon (:), drop a line, indent slightly and begin the quotation using inverted commas. This gives us:

Her clear-sighted sadness is seen in the words:

   'I have betrayed a great man, and his like will never be seen again.'

Sometimes your sentence will not describe the quotation but simply introduce it. In this case, the colon would only interrupt the natural flow of the words. So, instead, you should write:

Her clear-sighted sadness is seen when she comments that she has

   'betrayed a great man, and his like will never be seen again'.

Always make sure your longer quotations have room to breathe; drop a line (with or without a colon), indent slightly and add quotation marks. Drop another line before continuing your own text.

Shorter quotations

A good essay will have a mixture of longer and shorter quotations. Shorter ones can be just as effective as longer ones. If the longer quotation escapes you in full, you can use the remembered parts to great effect.

For instance, if you wanted to use the quotation

'the street shone out in contrast to its dingy neighbourhood, like a fire in a forest'

but you could not quite remember it in full, you could use the remembered phrases to good effect and paraphrase the rest.

The street is described as making a sharp contrast to its 'dingy neighbourhood' and standing out 'like a fire in a forest'.

As long as you weave the short quotations seamlessly into your own text, this kind of paraphrase-plus-quotation will prove more effective than a longer, misquoted extract. It may also pinpoint more sharply the exact point you wish to make.

GIVING A CONTEXT

There is a danger of assuming that readers understand more than they do. No quotation, however well chosen, will make its desired effect unless you give it a brief *context*. In other words, indicate briefly not just who said it but also why and under what circumstances it was said. If, for instance, you had been reading *Macbeth* and wanted to comment about King Duncan's generosity of nature, you might want to mention his kindness to a wounded messenger – but be careful how you do it.

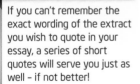

DON'T FORGET

If you can't remember the exact wording of the extract you wish to quote in your essay, a series of short quotes will serve you just as well – if not better!

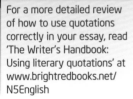

ONLINE

For a more detailed review of how to use quotations correctly in your essay, read 'The Writer's Handbook: Using literary quotations' at www.brightredbooks.net/N5English

Duncan shows he has a great generosity of nature:

   'Go get him surgeons.'

Duncan has a great generosity of nature. Seeing a badly wounded messenger collapse, he personally orders him to be taken care of:

   'Go get him surgeons.'

A context does not need to be long; it simply needs to lead readers into the quotation in a way that helps them to make sense of the point you are making.

ONLINE TEST

For more practice on perfecting your performance, test yourself online at www.brightredbooks.net/N5English

MAKING YOUR LEAD-IN WORK FOR YOU

Make sure your lead-in to the quotation does not simply repeat the content of the quotation. For example, in this description of *Buddha Da* by Anne Donovan, a bad lead-in would be:

Jimmy tells his wife he is going on a journey but he is not sure where he is going:

   'Ah'm on a journey but ah don't know where ah'm gaun.'

The lead-in here might better be:

Jimmy comes across to his wife – and to readers – as rather vague about his plans for taking his study of Buddhism forward:

   'Ah'm on a journey but ah don't know where ah'm gaun.'

In other words, a thoughtful lead-in does more than simply help the reader to understand the quotation's context; it can also underline your ability to evaluate its significance.

THINGS TO DO AND THINK ABOUT

It is difficult to identify exactly the moment when an examiner decides to award a top grade. There is an accumulation of factors at work here. These are some of the key ones which should be studied well in advance of entering the exam room.

- You need to demonstrate a thorough knowledge of your texts. That means reading them not just in class but regularly on your own as well.

- You must select *only* the information from your text knowledge which answers the specific question in front of you. Examiners do not want to know everything your teacher has taught you.

- You must be alert to all sections of the question and apportion your time accordingly.

- You need a plan to help you structure a coherent essay which is more than a loose collection of good points. There should be a line of argument that the examiner can follow easily as one paragraph flows smoothly into the next.

- Each paragraph should be carefully structured to ensure that your claims are borne out by evidence and that you unpack this evidence for the reader. In other words, you make a **S**tatement, back it up with **E**vidence and then give a **C**ommentary on it before moving on to the next paragraph (**SEC**).

- A soundly structured introduction will help you to stay on task, and a 'road-map' in the introduction's last sentence will help examiners to find their way round your arguments. A brief conclusion reminds them of your key points.

- Use the correct procedure for laying out quotations, long or short. This shows good academic manners and attention to detail that increases your stature as a competent commentator on your texts.

- Make sure that your quotations make sense. This means checking that you have given each one a context, however brief.

TRIAL ESSAY

Now that we've looked at all the bits and pieces that make up a critical essay, let's see what it looks like when we put it all together. Read through the essay, noting the various 'landmarks', and see if you can model your next critical essay on similar lines. Remember, there's no one approach to writing a critical essay; this is only one suggested line of thought.

> **Choose a short story or novel in which setting figures prominently.**
>
> **Describe the contribution of the setting and then show how this feature helped your understanding of the text as a whole.**

Note how underlined phrases pick up wording from the question.

Final two sentences of introduction suggest line of thought to be followed and the order in which evidence will be examined – and reference back to the wording of question.

Statement for SEC1

Start of Evidence for SEC1

Start of Commentary for SEC1

Line of thought highlighted

A novel in which <u>setting figures prominently</u> is *The Strange Case of Dr Jekyll and Mr Hyde* by Robert Louis Stevenson. Respectable Dr Jekyll, impatient with the restraints of respectability, longs to indulge in hidden, evil desires. To do so, he invents a potion which turns him into wicked Mr Hyde, thereby living out his dark side in another self. In Jekyll, the virtuous and the evil live side by side, just as in the novel's <u>setting</u> the attractive and the ugly co-exist in the world around him. By frequently drawing attention to the dual nature of the setting and setting several key events at night, Stevenson uses these features to help us understand what he is saying about the divided nature of Jekyll and his progress into his darker self.

In the opening chapter, Stevenson goes to great trouble to establish that the area around Hyde's laboratory home is a mixture of the prosperous and the dingy. We find that:

> 'the street shone out in contrast to its dingy neighbourhood, like a fire in a forest.'

It is presented as a particularly attractive, welcoming, street since

> 'the shop fronts stood along that thoroughfare with an air of invitation, like rows of smiling saleswomen'

and Stevenson notes its 'freshly painted shutters, well-polished brasses, and general cleanliness and gaiety of note.'

But Hyde's laboratory spoils this attractive setting, for

> 'a certain sinister block of building thrust forward its gable on the street.'

which

> 'bore in every feature the marks of prolonged and sordid negligence.'

The doorway itself was

> 'blistered and distained. Tramps slouched in the recess …'

Clearly then, Stevenson is suggesting that the area surrounding Jekyll is a curious mixture of the smart and the squalid. In other words, this is a neighbourhood whose identity is not clear-cut, one where the sordid cannot be separated from the attractive. <u>Given that Stevenson is suggesting elsewhere in the novel that man contains both the nasty and the virtuous within him, this split personality of the street helps us understand in a visual way that this split exists in society as well as in the individual. Stevenson may be hinting that Jekyll's divided personality is perhaps not unique.</u>

contd

But there is yet a further contrasting split of environments, for we later learn that this squalid laboratory building is connected to buildings in a nearby square. We learn that

> 'Round the corner from the by street there was a square of ancient, handsome houses, now for the most part decayed from their high estate.'

This decayed environment, however, is brightened by

> 'One house [which] wore a great air of wealth and comfort …'

This, it turns out, is the rather splendid home of Dr Jekyll. Stevenson is directing attention to the fact that there is a duality of identity in these very closely related environments: grubbiness rubs shoulders with the smart and attractive. This use of physical setting is key to our understanding of Stevenson's intentions here, for in this novella he is exploring Jekyll's claim that

> '… man is not truly one, but truly two.'

Jekyll believes that man has two sides to his nature: the decent, God-fearing, respectable side which his day-time life as Dr Jekyll represents; and the other, more sordid side of human nature, is the side drawn to the evil and corruption in which his night-time persona, Hyde, revels. <u>Just as sharply contrasting environments can exist side by side in towns and streets, so too can contrasting sides of human nature coexist in the same being. Jekyll, it is being discreetly hinted, is perhaps not unique; duality exists all around us, not just in human personalities but in society, too, as these contrasting but connected physical environments suggest.</u>

This split is given shape in one further way. While Jekyll's respectable medical life takes place by day, his activities as Hyde happen at night, underlining again a different kind of split setting. Key moments in the story take place at night. Enfield's first encounter with Hyde takes place in darkness at:

> 'about three o'clock of a black winter morning.'

The narrator, Utterson, only makes contact with Hyde at night; and one of Hyde's most vicious crimes, the murder of the MP Danvers Carew, also takes place at night. Jekyll's death and final transformation into Hyde takes place after midnight.

In a tale which explores the defeat of goodness in Jekyll's nature by his evil side, the setting of darkness is only fitting. Both goodness and evil originally lived side by side in Jekyll, but the goodness is gradually overtaken by the dark, just as day gives way to night. Darkness is, in the end, a useful setting for underlining the direction Jekyll's life increasingly takes.

Standing back from the text as a whole, we see that setting has been useful in helping understand it. We see that Stevenson has used contrasting townscapes to suggest that, just as it is difficult to separate the attractive and grimmer aspects of society, so it is with Jekyll – who may not be so different from the rest of us. As this is a tale which explores the darker side of human nature, it is only appropriate that evil frequently has darkness as a backdrop.

Statement for SEC2
Start of Evidence for SEC2
Start of Commentary for SEC2
Line of thought revisited
Statement for SEC3
Start of Evidence for SEC3
Start of Commentary for SEC3
Linking phrase to indicate start of conclusion
The underlined phrases act as a reminder to the examiner that you have fulfilled the task set out in the initial question.

CRITICAL READING: OVERVIEW

STUDYING DRAMA

WHAT'S INVOLVED?

Encouragingly, the skills you are acquiring for your RUAE work will serve you well again in the Critical Reading paper. Here again, your final score will be determined by:

- how well you *understand* what is going on in the text
- how well you *understand* what the question is asking you to do
- your ability to *analyse* how the author creates his/her effects
- your ability to *evaluate* the significance of the evidence presented.

Whether you are writing a critical essay on a class text or answering questions on a Scottish set-text, these are skills which you will draw on time and time again.

Successful Critical Reading, however, depends on one further important element. You need to be alert to the fact that the different genres which you are studying all have very different features. Drama, poetry, novels and short stories all have their own characteristics. Writing about or answering questions on these genres requires you to know what these differences are and how to respond to them appropriately in your essays and answers.

To help you do this successfully, let's take a look at some key points to help you identify the various genres.

STUDYING DRAMA: WHAT TO LOOK OUT FOR

In studying drama, we need to be alert to the fact that, unlike a novel, short story or poem, a play is much more than words on a page. Since it is meant to be acted out on a stage, we have to take into consideration all the resources writers have at their disposal to bring the narrative alive for the audience. The primary resource is, of course, dialogue between the characters. But in addition to this, we have to remember the contribution of stage presentation and stage directions, costumes, lighting, props, music, sound effects: all are vital to communicating a rounded experience to the audience. In short, when writing about or commenting on drama, don't limit your evidence simply to the text. Your available choice is much greater than that.

What to look out for in character presentation:

The cast	Their personality	How is this revealed?
Personal characteristics	What are the character's strengths?	• Dialogue with others • Speech characteristics • Soliloquies • Asides • Actions in key scenes • Costume • Stage directions
	What are the character's weaknesses?	
	How does the character view the world?	
	What motivates the character?	
Relationship to others	With whom is the character close?	• Dialogue • Speech characteristics • Soliloquies • Asides • Actions in key scenes • Costume • Stage directions
	With whom is the character in conflict?	
Development throughout the play	Does the character change over the course of the action?	Resulting from: • Own actions • Actions by others • Fate

contd

What to look out for in staging:

	Setting	How is this conveyed?
In the text	Where does the action take place?	• Stage directions
	In what period does it happen?	• Language/period references
	Over what time scale does the action take place?	• Time references
On the stage	What are the characters' social/financial situations?	• Stage decor • Stage props
	Do the characters' fortunes change?	• Costumes • Music/sound effects • Lighting

What to look out for in structure:

Exposition: setting the scene	This introduces us to the characters, their social situation and their relationships with each other.
Development: when things start to change	This usually happens when a new character arrives or something happens to change the existing situation.
Climax: as a result of growing tension	The development section is usually marked by emerging tensions between the characters, often precipitated by the arrival of the new character or changed circumstances. A crisis or confrontation will often painfully sweep away previously-held views of people or situations.
Resolution: a changed perspective	As a result of the crisis or confrontation, a new, clearer view of reality emerges. Previous misunderstandings or misconceptions are replaced, however painfully, by much more realistic appreciations of characters and relationships.
Key scenes: furthering understanding	These may happen at any point in the play. It is often in key scenes that we see the above situations being made clearer for the audience and the play's characters. It is in key scenes, too, that themes may clarify themselves and develop significantly.

What to look out for in themes:

	Possible material for themes	How is this revealed?
A theme is what the play is *about*. A plot is how this theme (or themes) is gradually revealed. A play may have several themes and sub-themes as the plot unrolls.	Personal relationships involving love/revenge/ambition/jealousy/etc.	• Dialogue • Soliloquies • Pairings • Confrontations • Key scenes
	Political engagement: what is being said about the outside world of great events as it affects the circle of the play's characters?	• Dialogue • Historical references • Reactions to historical events • Results of historical events
	Social theme: what is being said about the way people interact or react to society around them?	• Dialogue • References to social conditions • Effects on human behaviour

DON'T FORGET

When writing about or commenting on a play, don't overlook the evidence that comes from stage directions, lighting, costumes etc. A change of costume can be made to say a great deal about a character's changing fortunes; two characters at opposite ends of a family kitchen can say much about a relationship. Facts like this can sometimes be easier to memorise than a long quotation. And just as effective as evidence!

THINGS TO DO AND THINK ABOUT

Read again 'What to look out for in staging' then consider the opening scene of the play you are reading.

- Start to answer the questions in column two by thinking about the suggestions made in column three.
- Note down page references for the evidence you find. Often you will discover evidence in more than one place.
- Prepare your own personal comments on what this setting makes you feel about the characters' situation. You may want to repeat this exercise should the setting change at some point.

STUDYING PROSE

STUDYING PROSE: WHAT TO LOOK OUT FOR

In writing novels or short stories, writers all share one major aim: to create an experience for readers which mirrors exactly what the writer felt as he/she imagined the story. Their aim is the creation of a wholly convincing world in which readers lose themselves entirely until the very last page.

Unlike writers for the stage or film directors, writers of novels or short stories cannot call on lights, music, stage decor, special effects to create this all-absorbing experience. Words are their only tool, so imagery, word choice, sentence structure become vitally important in creating this world. Great care has to be given to ensure that characters and settings are created in such as way so as to come truly alive for the reader. We need to feel that we are *there* just as much as the characters and that these are characters we truly know, just as well as we know our friends and family. Being able to do this successfully is, published writers will tell you, as important as devising a clever plot. As we read, we will also become aware that the writer, through the characters, setting and plot, is saying something about the world they, and perhaps we also, inhabit. In other words, we will discover there is also a theme (or themes) holding the narrative together.

So let's look in some detail at what writers can do with characters, setting, plot and themes.

What to look out for in character presentation in novels and short stories:

Character	Things to consider
Role	<ul><li>Is he/she the narrator?</li><li>Is he/she the hero/heroine?</li><li>Is he/she the villain?</li><li>If neither narrator/hero/villain, why present in story?</li><li>What is his/her initial impact on the reader?</li><li>What creates this impact? Behaviour to others/treatment by others/author's description?</li><li>Does our view of him/her change?</li></ul>
Personality	<ul><li>What are his/her strengths?</li><li>What are his/her weaknesses?</li><li>Does he/she change throughout the action?</li><li>Age? Appearance?</li></ul>
Relationships	<ul><li>Who are his/her friends?</li><li>Does he/she *have* friends?</li><li>Is he/she contrasted with anyone else? What contrasts do you observe?</li><li>Is he/she in conflict with anyone? If so, who and why?</li></ul>
Behaviour in key incidents	<ul><li>How do his/her actions here reveal character?</li><li>What are his/her private thoughts here?</li><li>How do his/her actions affect others?</li><li>Are we told anecdotes about past behaviour?</li></ul>

contd

What to look out for in setting:

Setting	Things to consider
Physical	• When do the events happen? • Over what timescale? • Is landscape/townscape important to the narrative? • How do word choice, imagery and sentence structure contribute to the setting's description? • What changes of scene are there? • Are weather conditions important? • Does changing weather affect the morale of character? • Are there recurring references e.g. to heat, cold, water, colour etc.? Why might the writer have used these?
Society	• What level of society does the character find himself/herself in? Rich? Poor? Does this change? • What kind of society surrounds the character? Settled? Conflicted? • Does he/she fit in? • Does he/she encounter other types of society? How does he/she react to them?

What to look out for in plot:

Plot	Things to consider
Organisation	• Does the narrative unfold chronologically? • Does the narrative employ flashbacks? • Is there a cyclical movement? i.e. does the narrative end where it started? • Are all loose ends tied up?
Narrative style	• From whose viewpoint is the story told? The author? A character? • Is there more than one narrator? • How formal or informal is the narrator's tone? • Are there important action-provoking key scenes? Why are they important? What do we learn from them? What are the consequences for the characters – and the plot?

What to look out for in presentation of theme(s):

Theme	Things to consider
Social/historical	• What is being suggested about the society (or societies) described? Greedy, narrow-minded, prejudiced etc.? What evidence have you for saying this? • How does this evidence emerge? Key incidents/events? Conversations? Conflicts?
Personal/moral	• Are there personality characteristics that people may share in their dealings with others? What might these be? Generous, tolerant, repressed etc.? • What evidence have you for saying this? How does this evidence emerge? Key incidents/events? Conversations? Conflicts?

 DON'T FORGET

Make a decision early on in your novel or selection of short stories about how you are going to organise your revision file. Will it be by chapter/story? Or by character? Will you have a separate section for themes with page references for evidence? It is a good idea to make a decision on all this before you get too far into the text.

 THINGS TO DO AND THINK ABOUT

Once you have read a few chapters of your novel or several of your short stories, organise yourselves into four groups. One group (probably the largest) should look at key characters; one should look at setting; one should look at plot; a fourth group should look at theme(s).

Within each group, examine the second column of our grids on prose fiction and try to answer the questions which they pose about the short story or novel you are reading. Point to specific incidents/conversations/descriptions to support your answers (with page references).

Get a spokesperson to report your findings. Take notes to add to your revision file.

STUDYING POETRY

STUDYING POETRY: WHAT TO LOOK OUT FOR

Of all the genres you will study for National 5 poetry is perhaps the most difficult to define. A dictionary might tell you it is a 'literary work in which the expression of feelings and ideas is given intensity by the use of distinctive style and rhythm.' But this does not get us very far. What is certain, however, is that it is the most economical of genres. A moment, an idea, a feeling is brought to life in just a few lines. There is no room for vaguely selected words; each single word will be present either for its specific sound or associations; each combination of words forming metaphors, similes, alliteration, onomatopoeia etc is there to appeal not only to our intellects but also to our emotions and senses: sometimes touch, smell, taste and hearing as well as sight. The chosen rhythm will also add to the effect the poet is targeting.

You might like to ask yourself three questions about any poem which you may encounter:

- What is the poem about?

- What effect does it have on me?

- How has the poet created these effects?

The first question will require you to think about the theme of the poem: the challenges of love, the pain of regret, the pity of war or whatever you find it to be saying. The second question requires you to think about your personal reaction to the poem: amused, moved, surprised, perhaps provoked into thinking about something familiar in a new way. Your response to the first two will depend to a great extent on your answer to the third question: how did the devices and techniques of poetic language, rhythm and rhyme create a convincing experience for you? So, what are some of the forms, devices and techniques which you need to be on the look-out for?

What to look out for in form or structure

	Characteristics/effect	Example
Is it written in a set poetic form? Ballad, sonnet, ode etc.	A recognised poetic form with a pre-determined shape and regular rhyme scheme creates a tight framework for the poet's ideas and the reader's expectations. Often, the verses or **stanzas** within the framework will each deal with a specific aspect of the topic. Formality of this kind gives a reassuring sense of organisation to the topic.	*The king sits in Dumferline town,* *Drinking the blude-red wine:* *'O whare will I get a skeely skipper,* *To sail this new ship of mine?'* *O up and spake an eldern knight,* *Sat at the king's right knee:* *'Sir Patrick Spens is the best sailor* *That ever sailed the sea.'* 'Sir Patrick Spens', Sir Walter Scott
Is it written in free verse?	Here poets dispense with fixed patterns of rhythms and rhymes. Instead, to make their ideas memorable, they employ many poetic techniques such as alliteration, assonance, imagery, repetition, personification. Often they use enjambment to capture the rhythms of everyday speech.	*Through the ample open door of the* *peaceful country barn,* *A sun-lit pasture field, with cattle* *and horses feeding;* *And haze, and vista, and the far* *horizon, fading away.* 'A Farm Picture', Walt Whitman

contd

Techniques and devices to look out for

Here are some of the more common members of the figurative language family we have already looked at on page 17. These form the lifeblood of poetic language so are well worth looking at again. They fall broadly into two categories: those which conjure up visual pictures, and those which create pictures in sound – aural pictures, so to speak.

Visual imagery	Aural devices
Simile: a comparison between two items using 'like' or 'as'. *My love is like a red, red rose.* The effect of similes and metaphors is to add pictorial emphasis/impact to the written description.	**Alliteration:** the repetition of a particular consonant – or consonant sound – at the beginning of a group of words to create a certain sound effect. *Cold clay clads his coffin.* Here the harsh sound of the letter 'c' matches the grimness of the description. *Soft sighing of the southern seas.* Here the soft 's' sounds mimics the gentleness of the water's sound.
Metaphor: also a comparison but this time the two items being compared are not 'like' each other since one item becomes the other. *The eyes are window to the soul.*	**Assonance:** the repetition of a certain group of similar-sounding vowels in words close to each other, again used to create a certain aural effect. *And murmuring of innumerable bees.*
Personification: yet another way of making a comparison. Similes and metaphors can become examples of personification when an inanimate (without life) object is spoken of as if it were human and alive. *The kettle whimpers on a crazy hob.*	**Onomatopoeia:** here the sound of the word mimics its meaning. *Clink, fizz, rip, honk, boom, purr* suggest their meaning in their sound.
Hyperbole: an exaggerated image to create a certain effect (sometimes humorous) or to emphasise a point or intensify an emotion. *I'll love you, dear, I'll love you Till China and Africa meet.*	**Enjambment:** in poetry, this is the running on of one line into another or into several others, often to give either a conversational feel to the content or sometimes to suggest speeding up for an effect of urgency. It can also make the reader wait for a key point to be made when the sentence finally stops. *... for my purpose holds To sail beyond the sunset, and the baths Of all the western stars, until I die.*

DON'T FORGET

It is not enough to know the names of the various literary devices and to be able to spot them at work. You need always to be able to make a comment on how these devices *affected* you as a reader.

THINGS TO DO AND THINK ABOUT

If you wish to explore further the technical side of poetry, tap 'The Close Reading of Poetry uvic.ca' into your browser. This very readable and informative account will add usefully to your confidence when discussing poetry.

STUDYING POETRY (contd)

WHAT TO LOOK OUT FOR IN RHYTHM AND RHYME

The techniques and devices described in the previous section help create powerful sound effects. In poetry, sound is often as important as the meaning of the words in conveying the poet's intentions. If devices such as alliteration, assonance and onomatopoeia create what we might call the 'melody' of a poem, rhythm and rhyme help create the poem's underlying 'beat'.

ONLINE

Head to www. brightredbooks.net to explore further the technical side of poetry.

How can rhythm help me understand a poem?	How can rhyme guide my response to a poem?
1. Look for the stress pattern	Rhyme is when a poet deliberately repeats the end sound of certain lines to match the sound of other lines in a verse. We usually call this pattern a rhyme scheme. We identify it giving the end words the same letter:
A stress pattern in a line of poetry is a series of recurring stressed or unstressed syllables. The stress pattern in a line of poetry can often be helpful in understanding the mood of a poem:	

*I **leant** up*on *a **cop**pice **gate***
    *When **Frost** was **spec**tre **grey***
 *And **Win**ter's **dregs** made **des**olate*
    *The **weak**ening **eye** of **day.***
	There lived a wife at Usher's Well a
	 And a wealthy wife was she b
	 She had three stout and stalwart sons, c
	 And sent them o'er the sea b

('The Darkling Thrush', Thomas Hardy)	('The Wife of Usher's Well', Anon. Ballad)
The first syllable of the line is unstressed, the second stressed, which makes for a steady, movement forward. This deliberate pace suits and creates a thoughtful, reflective mood.	Even the very youngest children seem to derive pleasure from the sound of rhymes, as the lasting popularity of nursery rhymes suggests.
But here is a very different stress pattern and pace:	**1. Listen for the music**
***Fast**er than **fai**ries, **fast**er than **wit**ches,* ***Bridg**es and **hou**ses, **hedg**es and **dit**ches;*	One critic has suggested that 'Rhythm is the pulse of poetry, and rhyme is its echo.' Once you have detected the mood of the rhythm, you may find that the sound of the rhyme intensifies that mood. As such, rhyme supports rhythm to make a poem a musical as well as an emotional experience.
('From a Railway Carriage', R.L. Stevenson)	
This pattern of stressed and unstressed syllables, when said aloud, creates the fast rhythm of excited forward movement, very different indeed from the preceding reflective pattern.	**2. Look at the actual rhymes**
2. Say the lines aloud	Quite often, the *sense* of the words that perform the rhyme add much to the atmosphere of the verse. For instance, in the first poem in the column opposite: *grey* rhymes with *day*; *gate* with *desolate,* most of which emphasise a grim bleakness of mood.
Saying the words aloud helps you identify the pulse and pace of the lines. These, in turn, give you a strong 'feel' for what the poem might be about. Does the rhythm suggest a lively, or sad, or angry, or contented mood? For poets, rhythm is a basic tool for creating a multitude of moods and atmospheres.	

contd

How can rhythm help me understand a poem?	How can rhyme guide my response to a poem?
3. Look out for disturbances in the pattern	**3. Check for focus**
Sometimes, poets deliberately break the patterns they have set up to draw attention to a change of mood or atmosphere. This first verse below tells how a soldier in war follows orders and fires at the enemy. It follows a regular stress pattern:	Sometimes rhyme can concentrate the focus on a particular point to great effect.
But ranged as infantry, *And staring face to face,* *I I shot at him as he at me,* *And killed him in his place.*	*For sweetest things turn sourest by their deeds;* *Lilies that fester smell far worse than weeds.* ('Sonnet XCIV', William Shakespeare)
The next verse, however, has a broken, halting stress pattern, suggesting the soldier's growing doubt about his orders:	**4. Be aware of half-rhymes**
I shot him dead because — *Because he was my foe,* *J Just so: my foe of course he was;* *That's clear enough; although [...]* ('The man he killed', Thomas Hardy)	Sometimes poets like the framework of a rhyme scheme but do not wish the rhymes to dominate too much. They 'tone down' the rhyme by using half-rhyme at line ends to make the ends of lines less noticeable. A half-rhyme is a rhyme in which the rhyming words are close but not identical to each other. At times, poets will also use enjambment to add a conversational tone to these lines which are not 'end-stopped' by full rhyme.
	*When have I last looked **on*** *The round green eyes and the long wavering* ***bodies*** *Of the dark leopards of the **moon?*** *All the wild witches, those most noble **ladies**...* ('Lines Written in Dejection', W.B.Yeats)

THINGS TO DO AND THINK ABOUT

In considering the various literary genres you will be studying, always keep in mind:

- Different genres such as drama, prose and poetry all have different identifying characteristics.

- Discussing each genre requires you to think about how these differences will affect the evidence you produce in your essays and answers.

- Convincing essays and answers require knowledge of literary techniques; but they need much more than that; they need you to comment on *how* the techniques you noted affected your response as a reader. Never lose sight of that.

SCOTTISH LITERATURE IN NATIONAL 5

SCOTTISH TEXTS: WHAT'S INVOLVED?

Answering questions on a Scottish text which you have studied accounts for 20 of the 70 marks in the final exam. The skills which you are already acquiring as you work on Reading for Understanding, Analysis and Evaluation will again prove helpful here.

In the Critical Reading exam, you will be asked to read a short extract from your selected text(s) and answer a brief series of questions on the extract. As in RUAE, you will be asked to look at technical features such as word choice, sentence structure, tone, imagery and to demonstrate summarising skills. Here again, your final score will be determined by:

- how well you *understand* what is going on in the extract
- how well you *understand* what the question is asking you to do
- your ability to *analyse* how the author creates his/her effects
- your ability to *evaluate* the significance of the evidence presented.

In addition to all this, a final high-value question will ask you:

- to examine some particular feature of the extract
- to relate it to at least one other part of the text(s)
- to discuss similarities or differences in their commonality.

Do not be put off by the word 'commonality'. It is simply a technical term for seeing how a particular aspect of the extract relates to a feature(s) elsewhere in your chosen text(s) and discussing similarities or contrasts.

- In a play, novel, short story or poem, this aspect might be a theme as it is explored in the extract and elsewhere; **characterisation** variations/similarities in the extract and elsewhere; the language here (word choice, imagery, sentence structure, tone etc.) and as it appears elsewhere. This 'commonality' question might also ask you to relate how an idea, concern, challenge or problem encountered here is dealt with in the extract and in another area of the text(s).

- In a play, you need to be alert to all these and also to other key features such as stage directions, lighting, props, costume changes and changes of location. You need always to remember that a play is much more than words on a page: it is a combination of words, colour, sound, light and movement. These are rich areas for examining in an answer.

This Unit will be your guide in studying how best to optimise your performance. You will find four of the selected Scottish authors explored in some detail.

BOLD GIRLS, BY RONA MUNRO

Born in Aberdeen in 1959, the daughter of a radiotherapist and a Geology lecturer, Rona Munro was fascinated by playwriting from an early age. After studying at Edinburgh University, she quickly established herself as a rising star in drama circles with commissions for plays, screenplays and radio plays.

In a recent interview she underlined her interest in 'representing voices or people that have been under-represented' which, of course, is well illustrated in her portrayal of the four women here. In media terms, the wives, mothers and daughters of prisoners were the forgotten people of the Northern Irish 'troubles'.

At first glance, examining as it does the fallout from political turmoil, *Bold Girls* might appear to be overtly political, but Munro is keen to dispel this idea. In the same interview she remarked:

'If you put characters on stage that people are not familiar with seeing centre-stage or carrying a narrative, that is political. Just putting women centre-stage when I started out was a fairly political act. By making the audience have that act of empathy with someone whose experience isn't theirs is political. But within that I don't think plays should be arguing a case one way or another.'

Written in 1991, *Bold Girls* won Munro the 1991 London Critics Circle Theatre Award for Most Promising New Playwright. It is a powerful 'act of empathy' which deals with the everyday lives of four women, whose menfolk have been either killed or imprisoned for their roles in the 'troubles' in Northern Ireland.

DON'T FORGET

The page references in this section are from Hodder Gibson's 1995 edition of *Bold Girls*!

OUTLINE SUMMARY

The action takes place in the course of a late afternoon, evening and early morning in the West Belfast of what Munro, writing in 1991, calls 'today'. Three neighbours, Marie, Nora and Cassie, have their already difficult lives disrupted by the arrival of the mysterious young girl, Deirdre. Despite presenting the appearance of mutually supportive closeness, the trio pursue various consoling dreams which underline their isolation and which camouflage underlying tensions. Deirdre, in her search for the truth about her father, serves as a catalyst to revealing these cracks. Despite its many humorous moments, the play's searing examination of the stereotypical roles of men and women in the material-driven society of today gives it a significance which transcends Northern Irish boundaries.

ONLINE TEST

Take the '*Bold Girls*: An Introduction' test online at www.brightredbooks.net/N5English

THINGS TO DO AND THINK ABOUT

Look carefully at the opening scene's stage directions describing Marie's home. List the things we learn about Marie and her life before we even meet her.

ONLINE

Check out the multiple facets of Scottish literature. Go to '100 Best Scottish Books' at www.brightredpublishing.net/N5English

RONA MUNRO, *BOLD GIRLS*: CHARACTERS AND THEMES

CHARACTER STUDIES

Marie

'Cheerful, efficient, young' widow of Michael, whose image looks out on the living room. She overtly avoids any thought of a stain on his memory but is increasingly disturbed by the young girl in white who has begun to haunt her house as she tries to bring up her sons Mickey and Brendan to respect their father's memory. The picture of the Virgin Mary that hangs in her kitchen helps suggest her Christian values in the audience's mind before she even appears. She reacts with unquestioning generosity to Deirdre's arrival, in contrast to Nora and Cassie. She is regularly associated with acts of kindness to birds throughout the play, a kindness which finds its final expression in the welcoming into her home of Deirdre, seemingly her late husband's love child.

Cassie

Long-term friend of Marie is the 'sceptical, sharp-tongued' daughter of Nora, with whom she enjoys an uneasy relationship due partly to their conflicting views on Nora's dead husband and Cassie's father, Sean. The truth about Sean – violent brute of a husband or a man provoked beyond endurance by nagging – remains elusive throughout the play. She dreams of fleeing Belfast to start a new life, free from the drabness of provincial life and the guilt of knowing she had an affair with Marie's husband, Michael. This is a secret which emerges late in the play, partly due to the arrival of Deirdre. While Marie strives to maintain a rosy view of her late husband (but finally slashes his image when she accepts the truth of his rumoured infidelities), Cassie views her husband, Joe, with undisguised contempt. Joe's imminent release from prison is yet another reason for Cassie's wish to flee Belfast.

Nora

Source of much of the play's humour, Nora protects herself from the pain of a failed marriage, her judgemental daughter and the daily trials of living in strife-torn Belfast by retreating largely into a world of interior decoration. A victim of domestic and political violence, she is a rich source of stories told about her past experiences (which Cassie and Marie appear to have heard many times). Stories such as the one about the night she lost her bamboo suite to the British army and the arrest of her son-in-law Joe have been crafted by her into humorous yarns, her way perhaps of living with the pain of such incidents.

Deirdre

Emerges out of the 'darkness' of the violence around her, seeking the truth about her father, probably Michael, and the chance to come in from the cold, possibly by finding a home with Marie. Nurtured in violence, she has no qualms initially about revenging herself on society by stealing and destroying whatever comes to hand. Underneath this violence stemming from the dark places of her mind, she, like others in the play, clings to a consoling dream: the natural desire of a child for caring parents, recognition of her status as Michael's child and the security of a proper home. The play ends in the hope of a new life for her with Marie, perhaps the only dream in the play which is likely to be realised by events.

THEMES

Inequality of the sexes

According to Professor Douglas Gifford

'Munro's main theme is a satire on the way ordinary people live now – not just in Northern Ireland, but in the west, and indeed in any culture which imbalances the sexes in their social roles, encouraging stereotyping of male dominance and social privilege and female subservience to that behaviour.'

This we see in the way the men – who never appear – are pandered to by the women, even though from what we hear of their gambling, drinking, fighting and promiscuity, they are hardly worthy recipients of this attention.

The role of materialism

There is, however, another major theme which helps inform the action of the play. In Scene 2, Deirdre comments

The whole town's a prison, smash chunks off the walls 'cause we're all in a prison.

When we examine the lives of the three women, we see that Deirdre is not far from the truth. While a number of their men are certainly in Long Kesh prison, the women, too, are similarly confined, not simply in a society that privileges men, but in one where their lives are caught in a web of television game shows, films and soap operas and the cheapening materialism of peach-coloured polyester, Mickey's raspberry ice-cream syrup, magi-mixes and Black-and-Decker drills – the world of contemporary western culture, Munro seems to suggest.

But, it could be argued, this materialism is as much refuge as prison for these women as they struggle with the difficulties of reconciling their lives with a version of the truth with which they can live – one of the play's several sub-themes, which we will explore on the next page.

DON'T FORGET

When analysing drama, it is important to consider how the play's themes are conveyed not only through the characters' dialogue and interaction but through stage props, lighting, costume, setting and other stage effects.

THINGS TO DO AND THINK ABOUT

Read Douglas Gifford's full article, 'Making them bold and breaking the mould', at www.brightredbooks.net/N5English

ONLINE TEST

Take the *'Bold Girls*: An Introduction' test online at www.brightredbooks.net/N5English

RONA MUNRO: SUB-THEMES

THE TROUBLESOME TRUTH

Truth is always an elusive commodity – and nowhere more so than in this play. What *is* the truth behind Sean's violence towards Nora: a violent drunk or a good man provoked beyond endurance? And what are we to think of Joe, Cassie's husband? To Nora, he is a sound provider; to Cassie, a drunken oaf. To what extent exactly did Marie suspect her Michael of carrying on with other women? This difficulty in negotiating the truth drives the women into different positions.

Marie, whatever her suspicions, studiously <u>avoids confronting the truth</u>, telling her sons that

> *Your daddy was a good man and a brave man and he did the best he could and he's in heaven watching out for you and that's what [...] keeps me going, keeps me strong ...*

This mental image – and the physical image of Michael on the wall – comforts and sustains her as she goes about her life.

Cassie has spent some effort in <u>concealing the truth</u> about her relationship with Michael from Marie, which adds to her desire to escape what she sees as the grim, restricting provincial life of West Belfast.

Nora <u>flees the truth</u> of her bleak existence – her husband dead, a son in prison and herself the victim of military and domestic violence – by seeking comfort in maintaining and decorating her home, a trim retreat from reality. With a new roll of cut-price peach-coloured polyester, she is convinced <u>That'll be my front room just a wee dream again.</u>

Deirdre is the only one of the quartet who is actively *seeking the truth*: the truth about her paternity, a truth that will give her a home with Marie, she hopes, and allow her into a family life of the kind she has heretofore been deprived of, thereby escaping from the circle of violence and theft which seems to have been her life so far.

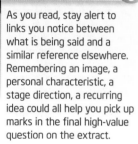

DON'T FORGET

As you read, stay alert to links you notice between what is being said and a similar reference elsewhere. Remembering an image, a personal characteristic, a stage direction, a recurring idea could all help you pick up marks in the final high-value question on the extract.

TALKING WITHOUT COMMUNICATING

There is no shortage of chat and banter in the play. Indeed, its robust interchanges are at the heart of the play's appeal. But there are various points in the play when we hear Marie, Cassie and Nora talking completely at cross-purposes, with no one really listening to anyone else. The effect can at times be humorous, as in the play's opening lines. But, at others, it emphasises the essential distance that exists between the women.

Despite a surface appearance of closeness and solidarity, they are essentially three lonely women who often fail in daily life to communicate to one another their doubts and fears. When they do, as happens in Scene 4, the results are disastrous, although it leads finally to a clearing of the air. This stifling of real communication is a sad but very necessary means of papering over the underlying cracks in the relationship between Marie and Cassie, and between Cassie and her mother. These recurring 'cross-talks' are one of Munro's ways of signalling their essential isolation in what appears to be a mutually-supportive quasi-family.

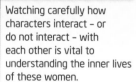

DON'T FORGET

Watching carefully how characters interact – or do not interact – with each other is vital to understanding the inner lives of these women.

Photo from the 1994 production of 'Bold Girls', at The Matrix Theatre, Los Angeles.

THE CONSOLING DREAM

To sustain them in their lives, the four women have forged their own consoling dreams. For Cassie, it is, Marie suggests, a dream of escape to Spain with a toyboy, hence her preoccupation with diets, her appearance in a bikini and the £200 she has stolen from Nora. Nora's dream, as we have seen, concerns escape into a world of peach-coloured polyester. Marie's dream is less materialistic, anchored as it is in a vision of Michael's essential goodness as she goes about tending to her family and feeding the birds. Deirdre, like Marie, is less materialistic in her dream, seeking a refuge from the streets into a family life of which she feels herself deprived. It is her 'wee bit of hard truth' which helps puncture the dreams of the other three; but there is, in the play's final pages, a hint that Marie and Deirdre may find consolation together, a consolation based on a reality stripped of distracting illusions.

 ## THINGS TO DO AND THINK ABOUT

For more insight into the setting of *Bold Girls*, read 'A Brief History of Belfast' at www.brightredbooks.net/N5English

 DON'T FORGET

When analysing drama, remember a play is not simply words on a page; it is a living thing, a performance in which ideas and themes come alive not simply through the characters' dialogue but also through the contribution of setting, clothes, music, lighting, props and stage effects. Keep this in mind when discussing the play. This is a play rich in hints from its stagecraft. Deirdre's knife and Michael's picture are just two. Think of others.

 ONLINE TEST

Take the '*Bold Girls*: Sub-Themes' test online at www.brightredbooks.net/N5English

RONA MUNRO: GETTING TO GRIPS WITH THE TEXT

DEALING WITH COMMONALITIES

Right at the beginning of this chapter, we defined in outline what a commonality question involves and suggested what the aim of the commonality-seeking final question is (See page 54). Once you have read several scenes of this play, you could usefully start practising the skills necessary for an effective answer. (In the upcoming Topic Test, you will be able to try answering a full commonality question on the extract.) But what exactly is a marker looking for in this kind of answer?

EXAMPLE:

Let's take a practice example. Suppose you were faced with a question similar to this:

This is a play in which women have to face up to many difficulties.
By referring to this extract and at least one other example from the play,
discuss what these difficulties are.   8

ANSWER:

The safest way to go about this is to adopt a simple formula.

Step 1: Say what difficulty arises in the extract (1 mark), then mention another difficulty faced in another part of the play (1 mark). This might read as:

Deirdre finds herself outside, frightened of the black smoke of a nearby violent explosion, showing the difficulty of living with sectarian violence. (1) The women's night out is later threatened when shooting in the street makes going out a problem. (1)

So we already have two marks.

Step 2: Now select a brief quotation from the extract which illustrates this difficulty (1 mark), then make your own comment on this (1 mark). This might read as:

'There's burning making the sky black.' (1) The women live with the constant threat of violence and/or explosions around them. (1)

So now we have four marks.

Step 3: Now find another quotation from elsewhere in the play which also illustrates a difficulty for the women, then add your comment on it.

'Wallop! Knocked her straight through the hedge'. (1) The women are sometimes victims of physical violence during raids. (1) (If you cannot remember a quotation from elsewhere in the play to illustrate a difficulty, refer in detail to the difficulty you have in mind and then comment on it.)

So now you have six marks.

Step 4: You now need some final reference/quotation to a difficulty and a comment.

'Oh, the paper's hanging off the wall in there.' (1) The houses they have to live in are poor quality, riddled with damp. (1) (Again, if you do not have the quotation to hand, refer to it in detail and then comment on the detail.)

And there are your eight marks.

From this exercise, you can see that the way to maximise your score is to know your text(s) thoroughly. You need to be able to make an instant mental survey of your text(s) and select appropriate material in very few minutes. This can only be done if your text knowledge is absolutely secure. That comes from multiple readings.

LET'S TRY THAT OUT

In this extract Marie and Cassie have returned from their night out at the club and are discussing their differing attitudes to coping with daily life.

CASSIE:	How do you stand it here, Marie?
MARIE:	Sure where else would I go?
CASSIE:	How do you keep that smile on your face?
MARIE:	Super-glue.
CASSIE:	There's not one piece of bitterness in you, is there?
MARIE:	Oh, Cassie.
CASSIE:	You see, you're good. And I'm just wicked.
MARIE:	Aye, you're a bold woman altogether.
CASSIE:	Is it hard being good?
MARIE:	I took lessons.
CASSIE:	Well, tell me what you've got to smile about, Marie, because I'm sure I can't see it.
MARIE:	I've a lot to be thankful for. I've my kids, my job, a nice wee house and I can still pay for it.
CASSIE:	You've two wee boys growing out of their clothes faster than you can get new ones, a part-time job licking envelopes for a wage that wouldn't keep a budgie and three red bills on your mantelpiece there.
MARIE:	That's what's great about a Saturday out with you, Cassie, you just know how to look at the bright side of things, don't you?
CASSIE:	Well, just tell me how you can keep filling that kettle and making folk tea without pouring it over their head?
MARIE:	Ah well you see, I'm a mug.
CASSIE:	I think you are.
MARIE:	I didn't marry Joe, but...
CASSIE:	No. You did not. That mug was me.
MARIE:	See, Cassie, I've had better times with Michael than a lot of women get in their whole lives with a man.
CASSIE:	And that keeps you going?
MARIE:	It's a warming kind of thought.

QUESTIONS

1 Marie demonstrates a range of responses to Cassie's criticisms of her life. With close reference to the text, explain what at least two of these are.   **4**

2 Cassie does not share Marie's positive view of her situation. With reference to word choice and/or sentence structure, explain clearly how Cassie regards it.   **4**

3 Men are held in low esteem by Cassie, although she appreciates how they may have their uses and attractions. With close reference to her language, show clearly two ways in which they might have attracted Cassie.   **4**

4 The extract refers to Marie's consolation in her difficult life. With close reference to the extract and at least one other place elsewhere in the text, explain how the idea of consolation is explored.   **8**

Total marks 20

ONLINE

Have a look at the 'National Library of Scotland's Description of *Bold Girls*' at www.brightredbooks.net/N5English

THINGS TO DO AND THINK ABOUT

Try out the questions above, then look at the hints on the next page and see how well you got on.

RONA MUNRO: SOME WAYS OF ANSWERING

How did you get on? Here are some pointers to possible answers and how to find them.

DON'T FORGET

In your exam, highlight or underline the portions of text from which you think your answers will come, then make your point based on what this quotation tells you.

HINTS FOR ANSWERS

Question 1

Various answers are possible but these are some that may be helpful.

Comment (×2) and textual reference (×2) required for four marks:

a) Matter of fact/logical:
- *Where else would I go?*

b) Flippant/humorous/witty:
- *Superglue*
- *Aye you're a bold woman altogether.*
- *I took lessons.*
- *I'm a mug.*

c) Embarrassed:
- *Oh Cassie!*

d) Reflective/thoughtful:
- *I've a lot to be thankful for.*
- *I've had better times with Michael than a lot of women get...*

e) Ironic:
- *you know how to look on the bright side of things...*

Question 2

Any comment (×2) plus reference (×2) for four marks from either category.

Word choice:

Boys... growing out of their clothes: suggests Marie cannot keep pace with increasing challenge.

Licking envelopes: suggests contempt/disdain for the low-skill/pettiness of the task.

Wage... wouldn't keep a budgie: exaggeration to show the tiny sum she earns.

Three red bills: suggests for all her efforts she is not managing her expenses.

Sentence structure:

Long sentence/list of problems which mount to a climax to lay out/illustrate/enumerate Marie's miserable/unfortunate circumstances.

Question 3

Comment (×2) and reference (×2) for four marks.

Word choice:

... good hands and warm skin..: physical appeal.

wrap him round you...: protective role like a warm coat to keep the rain off; useful as a barrier to life's problems.

smells like excitement....: gives off a strong aura/vibes of possibility of breaking with routine.

smells like escape: gives off a strong aura/vibes of possibility of being able to find a life elsewhere.

contd

By contrast, Amy is enchanted, particularly when she sees an addition to the nativity scene which she mistakes for an angel. The young man in question is clearly a homeless person but Sandra is reluctant to elaborate on the concept of homelessness to protect the child's innocence. Amy, however, seizes on the idea of offering the man a home with them. The child seems intuitively to understand the real spirit of Christmas in a way denied to the more worldly and practical adult.

Although a kindly and protective mother, Sandra seems cut off from the broader humanity of the child who reaches out instinctively to the homeless young man. Perhaps aware of her rather uncharitable attitude, Sandra offers three pounds to a passing paper-seller before mother and child make their way home on the bus, staring out 'intae the dark night.'

'HIEROGLYPHICS'

Mary Ryan lives in Drumchapel with her mother and sisters, Catherine and Elizabeth. She suffers from dyslexia and the isolation which this brings from her peers. Several half-hearted attempts are made at primary and secondary school to deal with her problem but to no avail.

We first meet her at the age of eight and follow her progress into lower secondary school. It's a throwaway insult from the unpleasant Mr Kelly which, ironically, opens a gateway to a new world for Mary: the language of hieroglyphics. Freed from having to use conventional methods of creating texts, she finds her own method of depicting her world and expressing her feelings – things that standard spelling and writing procedures have denied her. Through hieroglyphics, she rescues herself from marginalisation to participate in the world and work of her peer group.

ONLINE

You can enjoy another perspective on these stories by checking out 'The Short Review – *Hieroglyphics and Other Stories*' at www.brightredbooks.net

THINGS TO DO AND THINK ABOUT

When revising, make sure you have the characters' names and the story in which they appear at your fingertips. Knowing the story means being able to name the characters and their story quickly and accurately. Here's a quick test to remind you of some key names.

ONLINE TEST

Take the 'Anne Donovan: Stories under the spotlight' test online at www. brightredbooks.net/N5English

Characters	Name	Appearance in which story?
Girl with sharp intelligence who struggles with reading and writing.		
A girl whose mother appears not to love her.		
Girl who loved glitter pens.		
Woman who worked extra hours to make more money for Christmas.		
Girl who feels isolated from classmates.		
A girl with whom a heroine is unfavourably compared.		
A girl who feels compassion towards a homeless man.		

ANNE DONOVAN: GETTING TO GRIPS WITH THE TEXT

Be prepared to make connections of your own in this collection of fascinating characters and situations. In addition to uniting themes, there may well be family situations, personal difficulties, narrative styles, language choices about which you could make sound points in a commonality question. To pick up top marks for this, it's vital to know the connections between the stories.

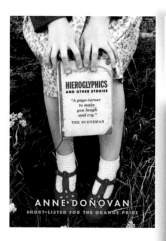

LET'S TRY THAT OUT

Read the extract below and then attempt the following questions.

'Hieroglyphics' by Anne Donovan

Anither brand new jotter. Anither set a rules tae copy. This is the last period a the day and the sixth time ah've hud tae dae it. Could they no jist huv wan lot a rules fur every class? It takes me that long tae copy the rules oot that the lesson's nearly finished and ah've missed it. The French teacher took wan look at the dug's
5   dinner ah wis producing and tellt me no tae bother. And the Maths teacher asked me ma name an looked me up in a list.

You're Mary Ryan, are you? Mmm.

Must of been the remmy list. Ah'm no remmy at Maths right enough – it's jist ah cannae read the stuff. If sumbdy tells me whit tae dae ah kin usually dae it, ah
10   jist cannae read it masel in thae wee booklets. It's funny how the numbers never seem tae birl aroond the way the letters dae; mibby it's because there urny usually as many numbers in a number as there are letters in a word, if ye know whit ah mean. Or is it because ye read them across the way and ye dae Maths doon the way? Mibby if ah lived in wanny thae countries where they wrote doon the way
15   ah'd be aw right. Ah mean no evrbdy writes like we dae. We done a project on it in Primary Five and there's aw kinds a ways a writin in the world. Some folk read right tae left and some up and doon. And they Egyptians drew wee pictures fur aw their writin. Ah hink ah should of been an Egyptian.

And what's this supposed to be – hieroglyphics?

20   Ah hated that sarky bastard, Mr Kelly. Skelly, we cried him though he wisnae actually skelly; he used tae squint at ye through wan eye as if he wis examinin ye through a microscope an hid jist discovered some new strain a bacteria that could wipe oot the entire population a Glasga. He wis the Latin teacher but he hud hardly oany classes because naebdy done Latin noo so they'd gied him oor class
25   fur English, and then every time a teacher wis aff sick he used tae take the class, so ah began seein a loaty him. And that wis bad news.

Ye see ah'd never felt like this afore wi oany ither teachers. Ah knew whit they were thinkin of me right enough, ah could see it in their eyes, but maisty them jist thoat ah wis a poor wee sowl that couldnae learn oanythin, so whit wis the
30   point a them tryin tae teach me? Sometimes they even said it oot loud, like when the heidie wis his wee dauner roon the classes tae make sure we were aw workin hard and no writin graffiti on wer jotters. (Chance wid of been a fine thing.)

And how are they settling in, Miss Niven?

contd

35 *Oh very well, Mr McIver, they're all working very hard on their projects on the Egyptians. Amir has produced a wonderful imaginative piece on the last thoughts of Tutenkhamun and look how neatly Mary's coloured in the borders of the wall display.*

She's a poor wee soul but she tries hard.

Obviously no bein able tae read makes ye deif.

But that big skelly bastard wis different. Tae start wi ah thoat he wis jist borin
40 and boredom is sumpn that disnae bother me, ah'm used tae it, ah hink maist weans are. The furst few days he rambled on aboot grammar and wrote stuff up on the board an we didnae really huvty dae oanythin bar keep oor mooths shut. Which is easie-peasie tae me. But then he startit tae dictates notes tae us and he could time his pace jist so. If ye kin imagine the class like a field a racehorses then
45 he wus gaun at such a pelt that only the furst two or three could keep up wi him. The rest wur scribblin furiously, their airms hingin oot thur soackets, sighin an moanin ower their jotters, and then he'd tease them wi a pause that wis jist a toty bit aff bein long enough tae let them catch up, an then, wheech, he wis aff again lik lightning.

50 Me, ah wis the wan that fell at the furst fence.

QUESTIONS

1 Look at paragraph one. ('Anither brand... in a list.')
   Show two examples of Anne Donovan's language which suggest Mary's
   frustration with classroom administration.   4

2 Look at paragraph three. ('Must of been... an Egyptian.')
   Explain using your own words as far as possible why Mary feels success is more
   possible for her in Maths than in English. You should make two main points.   2

3 Using your own words as far as possible, summarise Mary's reasons for disliking
   Mr Kelly. You should make four main points.   4

4 Look at the final paragraph. ('But that big skelly... furst fence.')
   Explain how any one example of the writer's use of language in these lines
   reveals that Mary, despite self-doubts about her writing ability, is a skilled
   observer of classroom life.   2

5 Young girls in Donovan's stories are often faced with difficulties in their lives.
   With reference to this extract and to at least one other story, show how these
   difficulties are explored.   8

   Total – 20 marks

THINGS TO DO AND THINK ABOUT

How did you fare in question 5? This is the first time where you had to link your appreciation of *this* text to another text altogether. You will have seen that, to answer this high-value question successfully in the exam, you really need to know your short stories very well indeed. In the exam, you won't have the texts in front of you to look back for similarities and differences as you do now!

DON'T FORGET

Be prepared to make connections of your own in this collection of fascinating characters and situations. In addition to uniting themes, there may well be family situations, personal difficulties, narrative styles, language choices about which you could make sound points in a commonality question. To pick up top marks for this, it's vital to know the connections between the stories.

ONLINE

Check out 'The Short Review – *Hieroglyphics and Other Stories*' for another perspective on the collection at www.brightredbooks.net/ N5English

ANNE DONOVAN: SOME WAYS OF ANSWERING

HINTS FOR ANSWERS

Characters	Name	Appearance in which story?
Girl with sharp intelligence who struggles with reading and writing.	Mary Ryan	'Hieroglyphics'
A girl whose mother appears not to love her.	Alison	'Dear Santa'
Girl who loved glitter pens.	Clare	'All that Glisters'
Woman who worked extra hours to make more money for Christmas.	Sandra	'Away in a Manger'
Girl who feels isolated from class mates.	Mary	'Hieroglyphics'
A girl with whom a heroine is unfavourably compared.	Katie	'Dear Santa'
A girl who feels compassion towards a homeless man.	Amy	'Away in a Manger'

Question 1

Any two of the following possible answers.

- *Anither brand new jotter. Anither set a rules tae copy.* (1) The two minor sentences in quick succession foreground Mary's sense of irritation at what she sees as needless waste of time and effort. (1)

- *Anither [brand new jotter]...Anither [set a rules]* (1) The repetition of 'anither' emphasises that Mary was extremely conscious of the growing number of rules. (1)

- *Could they no jist huv wan lot a rules fur every class?* (1) The rhetorical question underlines Mary's exasperation at what she sees as needless duplication. (1)

Question 2

Any two of the following points.

- She can follow the verbal instructions when they are given in Maths.

- Numbers in Maths, unlike letters in English, do not move around in front of her eyes.

- There are fewer figures in a number than letters in a word.

- She believes the vertical rather than horizontal nature of Maths may make the reading of it easier for her.

Question 3

Any four of the following possible answers.

- He was sarcastic.

- He viewed her as if she was a dangerous microbe/as if she was not human.

- He dictated notes too fast.

- He lacked consideration for the class.

- She was totally incapable of keeping up with his dictation.

contd

Question 4

Any two of the following possible answers.

- *like a field a racehorses* (1): the simile suggests the great pace which the pupils had to maintain to keep up with Mr Kelly's dictation. (1)

- *their airms hingin oot thur soackets* (1): the exaggeration/hyperbole gives an imaginative picture of the distress of the class. (1)

- *aff again like lightnin.* (1): the simile emphasises the speed at which Mr Kelly would take off after a teasing pause. (1)

- *fell at the first fence* (1): Mary sees herself as an early casualty in this classroom activity which she describes graphically in horse-racing terms. Emphasised by the use of alliteration on 'f'. (1)

- The extended metaphor taken from horse-racing *a field of racehorses/gaun at such a pelt/keep up wi him/let them catch up/aff again* underlines Mary's imaginative creativity in describing what is going on in the class. (2)

Question 5

- Mary Ryan in 'Hieroglyphics' has to deal with the difficulties posed by dyslexia. (1) Clare in 'All That Glisters' has the difficulty of marking her father's passing in her own way by wearing the clothes he would have liked. (1)

- *It takes me that long tae copy the rules oot that the lesson's nearly finished and ah've missed it.*'(1) Mary's dyslexia makes writing so time-consuming she misses out on the work of the class. (1)

- *Whit the hell dae you think you're daein? Go and get changed this minute.* (1) Clare's aunt responds hostilely to Clare's choice of bright clothes for the funeral, even though they were her father's favourites. (1)

- *Ma mammy disnae love me.* (1) Alison's difficulty in 'Dear Santa' is that she feels her mother does not love her and struggles to attract her affection. (1)

 THINGS TO DO AND THINK ABOUT

1 In Mary Ryan's long struggle towards self-expression, what was the contribution of each of the following towards that?

   (a) The 'remmy wumman'

   (b) Miss Niven

   (c) Mr Kelly

   (d) Mary herself

2 With a partner, discuss who contributed most and who contributed least to Mary's breakthrough.

3 What view is Anne Donovan gently hinting at here about education's ability to support pupils facing learning challenges?

EDWIN MORGAN

MORGAN: THE MAN

Born in 1920 in Glasgow, Edwin Morgan attended Rutherglen Academy and Glasgow High School before entering Glasgow University in 1937. He read English Language and Literature there until his studies were interrupted by the Second World War, when he enrolled as a conscientious objector in the Royal Army Medical Corps.

He returned from service in the Middle East to complete his degree with First Class Honours. On graduating, he took up a post at the university, where he taught until he retired in 1980 as titular professor of English to devote the rest of his life to writing. He was the recipient of many honours, including the Queen's Gold Medal for Poetry in 2000. He was appointed Scotland's first 'Scots Makar' of modern times, the Scottish equivalent of Poet Laureate, in 2004. He died in 2010.

MORGAN: THE POET

Morgan was among the most inventive, adventurous poets of his age, seeing poetry 'as an instrument of exploration, like a spaceship, into new fields of feeling or experience'. The poems you study for National 5 give only a minuscule indication of the depth and breadth of his output.

EXAMPLE:

Here is an example of Morgan's concrete style at its most playful. The poem is called 'Siesta of a Hungarian Snake'. This is the whole poem.

s sz **sz** S̲Z̲ **sz** S̲Z̲ **sz** Z̲s̲ **sz** Z̲S̲ **sz** zs z

In terms of language, he ranges widely from Glaswegian Scots to attempts to create the language of the Loch Ness Monster, men from Mercury, Hungarian snakes or even an African hyena. Complementing this desire to give a voice to others is a drive to intensify the power of his own, often through a series of complex verbal effects – a process which appears to have fascinated him and which we see at work in several of the poems for study here. In terms of topics, he ranges widely, often finding material in his native Glasgow or in the history and geography of Scotland, but also venturing into the worlds of computers, interplanetary travel, Bible history or even pre-history.

THE POEMS

'Good Friday'

There is a 'me' in this poem, presumably Morgan himself, who restricts himself to giving the time and place of the encounter; but the poem is essentially a dramatic monologue by a cheerily drunken man who, in the course of a brief bus journey along Bath Street in Glasgow, comments on Christ's crucifixion and resurrection, the meaning of Easter, his own drinking habits, lack of education and immediate intentions. At what is usually a time on Good Friday (3pm) when, historically, a darkness was said to cover the land, this Glasgow Good Friday is bathed in sunshine, and the tipsy man is happily celebrating and off to buy Easter eggs for the *kiddies*. Morgan cleverly captures the speech patterns of the man which, like the bus itself, are given to lurches and sudden changes of direction. Note how Morgan avoids any direct comment on his fellow traveller but listens uncritically and seems to find the man's chatter inoffensively amusing, even picturing his descent from the top deck in 'concrete' terms, with a word for each descending step.

VIDEO LINK

Follow the link 'Off the page: Edwin Morgan', at www.brightredbooks.net/N5English, for a very useful 25-minute film in which Morgan discusses his life and the development of his writing. He also reads some of his own poetry, against the background of Great Western Road, Glasgow, mentioned in the poem 'Winter' here.

contd

'In the Snack-bar'

Here, as in 'Good Friday', we have another casual Glasgow encounter. There are, however, sharp differences: this time the effect is far from cheery and light-hearted as before; this time the speaker, again presumably Morgan, describes the setting, the action and his response to it. In a detailed realisation of a *crowded evening snack-bar* with its formica, hissing coffee machine and fixed stools, the old man is presented almost as a species from another world, *like a monstrous animal caught in a tent/In some story*. The speaker helps the old man go to the toilet. Skilfully, Morgan captures the slow progress of the pair as they descend the stairs to the toilet by effective use of repetition and inversion:

And slowly we go down. And slowly we go down.

This is a technique which Morgan returns to several times in the poem to mirror the man's painfully slow progress in carrying out any action. His helplessness and clumsiness in coping with the simplest action is frequently further underlined by Morgan's word choice: *he shambles uncouth, he clings to me, to haul his blind hump.* Morgan is not only an active, compassionate helper here (one whose strength serves to emphasise the frailty of the old man) but also a moved, distraught commentator:

Dear Christ, to be born for this!

'Trio'

While 'In the Snack-bar' records the darker side of city life in Glasgow, in 'Trio' we see Morgan delighting mightily in a casual encounter in Buchanan Street one 'sharp winter evening' just before Christmas. Here the speaker, like the drunk man in 'Good Friday', appears to have doubts as to the credibility of the Christian myth (*Whether Christ is born, or not born …*). Nevertheless, there is no doubting the sheer joy that the trio of two young girls and a young man inspire in the speaker as he describes in great detail their sighting, the gifts they carry and the *cloud of happiness* that surrounds them. Morgan is here cleverly using these three young people and their surroundings to draw modern-day parallels with the three kings of the Christmas legend: they carry gifts, not the gold, frankincense and myrrh of the Magi, but a guitar, baby and chihuahua; they appear, not under a star but under the Christmas lights of Buchanan Street; a child, too, is central to the encounter.

The speaker dips into yet another myth (of Orpheus and his lute) to salute in mock-heroic terms the mistletoe of the guitar-carrying young man as an *Orphean sprig*, hailing also the baby and chihuahua in equally delighted exclamations of joy. This happiness may be the outcome of a commercially-driven Christmas rather than a religiously-inspired one, but the speaker sees it having the power, no less than a Christian one, to drive away the gloom of *the vale of tears* which is the world, and which *abdicates/under the Christmas lights*. It is a joy which lingers even after they have passed out of sight, marking the *end of this winter's day*.

Morgan employs a contrast of styles here: in the early lines his language is matter-of-fact, conversational in its use of enjambment and simple word choice to describe the physical appearance of the trio. Then, with *Orphean sprig!*, Morgan seeks to underline the significance he places on this encounter by adopting a more rhetorical, lofty tone and language as he mulls over its lasting power to inspire. What began as a snapshot of three ordinary young people carrying Christmas gifts in a Glasgow street ends as a more philosophical celebration of the great power of joy to enrich the lives of those observing it.

DON'T FORGET

When exploring a poem, being able to pick out language features such as imagery, word choice or sentence structure is important, but it is not the whole story. Being able to comment in your own words on the effect each technique has on the reader is equally important.

ONLINE TEST

Take the 'Edwin Morgan' test online at www.brightredbooks.net/N5English

THINGS TO DO AND THINK ABOUT

In class, you will be reading these poems from the various Morgan collections. For your own revision purposes, it might be useful to type them out. In this way, you can underline/highlight words and phrases and connect them to your notes in the margin. Revising will be that much easier when you have notes/comments/quotations all side by side.

EDWIN MORGAN (CONTD)

'Winter'

Here Morgan exploits his English lecturer's knowledge of Tennyson's 1833 poem 'Tithonus', a man who in Greek mythology sought immortality but forgot to wish for eternal youth as well. Tennyson's poem begins:

> *The woods decay, the woods decay and fall,*
> *The vapours weep their burthen to the ground,*
> *Man comes and tills the field and lies beneath,*
> *And after many a summer dies the swan.*

Tithonus is, consequently, left as a lonely, solitary character, a fate which seems to be shared by the speaker here as, at the end of the poem, he gazes at the *grey dead pane*. Is that *pane* a play on 'pain'? By altering the punctuation subtly, Morgan achieves a complex verbal effect in his opening lines, drawing as he does the reader away from classical Greek myth and Tennyson to his own more mundane world of Great Western Road and Bingham's Pond, local home of mute swans.

contd

The altered punctuation leads in its shortened phrases to a fractured forward movement, far from the smoothly-flowing melancholy of the earlier poem. The halting progress continues in the fragmented phrases as Morgan describes the frozen winter scene, insisting on hardness and sharpness as *swan-white glints only crystal beyond white*. This is intensified as the *stark scene* is *cut* by *cries in the warring air* and the *hiss of blades*. The harshness of the alliteration and onomatopoeia only add to the bleakness.

Gradually, the skaters disappear into the fog as, eventually, do the lights themselves. Now the scene is left to the fog which takes over and *drives monstrous down the dual carriageway* like some demonic driver, leaving the speaker solitary, staring blankly at only greyness. And greyness stares back at him. In its rich poetic effects which underline the bleaker aspects of winter, this is a poem in which the speaker's emotions seem as frozen as the external landscape.

'Glasgow Sonnet No 1'

The sonnet is a 14-line poetic structure most commonly used in the past for poems of love and romance. Here, Morgan harnesses it to a much bleaker task. Camera-like, the poet's description moves relentlessly in from a broad focus on the *backcourt* in the first quatrain (four lines) to an increasingly narrower one until it alights, finally, on the unemployed man. The second quatrain moves upwards from the courtyard onto the building itself. The mother and daughter seem besieged in the crumbling building, with only a *cracked sill* to buttress them against their hostile environment. So grim is the scene that even *The kettle whimpers on a crazy hob*. The final three lines arrive at the bedside of the sick, unemployed man. The focus has moved steadily from a wide exterior angle to a close-up focus on this figure of despair coughing out his life. From urban desolation, we have moved on to its human counterpart, a man as derelict as the building he inhabits.

'Glasgow 5 March 1971'

This is a poem which, like 'Trio', features a city-centre street encounter, but here the stark brutality of the scene highlights a very different side of city life. Morgan uses this 'moment-in-time' technique, however, to present us with more than a simple snapshot; we are offered a thought-provoking image which says much about Morgan's society which, some might say, has changed very little since 1971.

The poem is structured around three couples: the two victims of the attack, the two thieving thugs and the two passing drivers. The frequent use of enjambment throughout the poem helps establish an almost conversational tone, seemingly at odds with the horrific nature of the attack. At moments, however, his word choice bursts out of this matter-of-fact, black and white language to underline the horror of the moment with graphic vividness.

On a sharp clear night in the centre of town, a young couple is being used as a battering ram by *two youths* to smash a shop window in order to steal goods. Morgan's methodical description comes most vividly alive when he describes the actual violence, when we hear that the young man's beard, horrifically, is bristling not with stubble but with *fragments of shattered glass* and the girl's leg, caught on the shattered window *spurts arterial blood/over her wet-look white coat*. In contrast, the thugs are described matter-of-factly as they *are about to complete the operation [...] Their faces show no expression*. This act of savagery is to them merely an *operation*. Meanwhile, two passing motorists, good drivers but poor citizens, *keep their eyes on the road*. Morgan's meaning is clear: witnesses to such acts (perhaps readers included) do not wish to become involved. And so violence in society continues. Powerfully, Morgan makes no direct comment, leaving the snapshot to speak for itself.

ONLINE

Discover more about Edwin Morgan and his poems by clicking 'Scottish Poetry Library: Edwin Morgan Archive' at www.brightredbooks.net/N5English

ONLINE TEST

Take the 'Edwin Morgan: The Poems' test online at www.brightredbooks.net/N5English

THINGS TO DO AND THINK ABOUT

Try to find the ASLS-issued CD *17 Poems of Edwin Morgan,* which also has 'Trio' and 'In the Snack-bar' with a commentary by Professor Roderick Watson.

EDWIN MORGAN: GETTING TO GRIPS WITH THE TEXT

ONLINE

For more resources on Morgan, check out 'Education Scotland: Edwin Morgan poems' at www.brightredbooks.net/N5English

'GLASGOW SONNET NO. 1'

A mean wind wanders through the back court trash.
Hackles on puddles rise, old mattresses
puff briefly and subside. Play fortresses
of bricks and bric-a-brac spill out some ash.
5 Four storeys have no windows left to smash,
but the fifth a chipped sill buttresses
mother and daughter the last mistresses
of that block condemned to stand, not crash.
Around them the cracks deepen, the rats crawl.
10 The kettle whimpers on a crazy hob.
Roses of mould grow from ceiling to wall.
The man lies late since he has lost his job,
smokes on one elbow, letting his coughs fall
thinly into an air too poor to rob.

QUESTIONS

1 Look at the first four lines of the poem. By referring to two examples of imagery, explain how they help make these lines an effective opening to the poem. **4**

2 Look at lines 5–8. By referring to one example of the poet's use of language, explain fully how the poet makes clear how the building and its tenants seem to be under threat. **2**

3 Look at lines 9–11. By referring to two examples of the poet's use of word choice or imagery, explain fully how the poet makes clear the disturbed nature of life in the flat. **4**

4 Look at the poem's last line. Explain, referring to the words 'air too poor to rob', why they make an effective close to the poem. **2**

5 In Morgan's poetry the challenges of city-centre life are a recurring theme. By referring to this poem and to at least one other poem by Morgan, show how the poet uses word choice and/or imagery to explore this theme. **8**

Total marks 20

HINTS FOR ANSWERS

Question 1

Any two of the following. Possible answers include:

A mean wind wanders (1): the personification of the wind is startling, making it sound like an intruder (1)/the 'meanness' of the wind suggests an upcoming threat (1)

Hackles on puddles rise (1): hackles are more usually associated with cats or dogs, so it is arresting to hear them associated metaphorically with puddle. (1)/the fact that hackles have risen might suggest that there might be a metaphoric threat/menace in the offing (1).

Old mattresses puff (1): the personification of the mattresses makes them seem alive, leading a life of their own where no human thing seems to be moving (1).

Question 2

Any one of the following. Possible answers include:

No windows left to smash (1): the total destruction of the windows on the first stories suggest the building has been under determined attack (1).

A chipped sill buttresses (1): the fact that the women need the defence/support of the sill suggests they are besieged in some way (1).

The last mistresses (1): the fact that there are to be no more people in charge of the building suggests that its final days are not far off (1).

contd

Question 3

Any two of the following. Possible answers include:

Cracks deepen (1): the fabric of the building seems to be splitting around them as they go about their business, a far from normal situation (1).

Rats crawl (1): the fact that rodents are invading their home suggests all is not at all well here (1).

Kettle whimpers (1): the personification of the kettle, seemingly crying, suggests a disturbed departure from the normal nature of things. Usual personification traditionally sees kettles singing (1).

A crazy hob (1): 'crazy' is a powerful word since it suggests that even an inanimate object has been driven out of its mind by the state of the home (1)/'crazy' could also refer to the hob tilting because of the sloping angle of the decaying building (1).

Question 4

Any one of the following. Possible answers include:

There was a reference to a prowling *mean wind* at the start of the sonnet; the reference to *air too poor to rob* at the end gives a satisfying cyclical shape to the poem. It couples opening reference to 'wind' with closing reference to 'air'. (2)

In the opening line, the threat inherent in the *mean wind* which wandered, almost like a predator, into the backcourt, making the puddles hackles rise, is dismissed in the final line. There is clearly nothing here (including its air) worth robbing (if robbery was its original intention).

Question 5

The poems which deal with misery to be found in city-centre life and which could be cited in addition to this one to answer the question are 'In the Snack-bar' and 'Glasgow 5 March 1971'.

A cited word choice/image is worth 1 mark; a full comment on the cited word choice/image is worth 1 mark.

Possible word choice/images include:

'Glasgow Sonnet No 1' (challenges here are human isolation and desolation in a derelict, poverty-stricken landscape.)

A mean wind wanders/hackles on puddles rise/a cracked sill buttresses/the kettle whimpers on a crazy hob/an air too poor to rob (others are also possible)

'In the Snack-bar' (challenges here are isolation in modern city life of the 'other'/those who face the challenges of disability.)

like a monstrous animal caught in a tent/... down two flights of steps, but we go/he clings to me./he shambles into the clinical gleam/the faltering, unfaltering steps/wherever he could go it would be dark/his life depends on many who would evade him (others are also possible)

'Glasgow 5 March 1971' (challenges here are victimisation through violence and society's apparent apathy towards it.)

bristling with fragments of glass/spurts arterial blood/arms are starfished out/keep their eyes on the road (others are also possible)

DON'T FORGET

Make sure that you take note of the marks which each question carries, and judge your time appropriately.

THINGS TO DO AND THINK ABOUT

By now, you should be getting into the habit of supporting your answers to these types of question with carefully selected evidence from the text. You may have a perfectly intelligent and sensitive response to the poem, but if it is not backed up by detailed references to the text (where requested) or in your own words (where requested), you will fail to achieve the marks you are aiming for. Make sure, too, that you take note of the marks which each question carries, and judge your time appropriately.

ROBERT LOUIS STEVENSON, *THE STRANGE CASE OF DR JEKYLL AND MR HYDE*

ROBERT LOUIS STEVENSON

Son of a famous engineer, Robert Louis Stevenson was born on 13 November 1850 in Edinburgh.

A victim of ill-health from his childhood, he spent as much time as possible away from the harsh Scottish weather. By the 1870s he was beginning to have some success as a writer, a fact which allowed him to travel extensively in Europe. While travelling in France he met the American who was later to become his fiercely protective wife.

1886 was a breakthrough year for the writer when his short novel or novella *The Strange Case of Dr Jekyll and Mr Hyde* was published to great acclaim. In the same year, he had another success with *Kidnapped*. Literary success allowed him to travel to warmer climates for his health. Enjoying travel in the South Pacific, he visited many of the islands, including Tahiti and Hawaii, before settling finally in Samoa where he died suddenly on 3 December 1894.

BACKGROUND TO THE NOVEL

Although a resident of Edinburgh's prosperous New Town, the young Stevenson enjoyed spending his leisure time in the more disreputable Old Town, where the constraints of respectable society were far less limiting. No stranger to wild nights in the Old Town's drinking dens, he would return in the early hours to the respectability of the family home. But in pursuing two contrasting lifestyles in nineteenth-century Edinburgh, he was by no means unique. As a native of Edinburgh, he would be familiar with the tale of the eighteenth-century Edinburgh town councillor Deacon Brodie, who led a double life as a respectable cabinet-maker by day and as a burglar by night in order to fund his gambling habit and mistresses. In short, Stevenson would be no stranger to ideas of a divided self, the starting point for the novella which we are studying here.

But the divided self was by no means a phenomenon which demonstrated itself in civic life solely in Edinburgh. In Victorian middle and upper-class society at large, outward morality and respectability were highly prized. But behind this upright facade, personal instincts and behaviour were often quite different. In the back streets of cities like London, crime and various forms of moral depravity flourished. In polite society, any direct reference to such unpalatable truths would be hypocritically repressed, as indeed they are by Utterson and Enfield in the opening chapter. They may suspect much, but they say little. Comment, like society itself, appears repressed throughout.

The idea of the divided self (sometimes referred to as 'duality') crops up in many places in this text – and not simply in the character of Dr Jekyll. Look out for this duality in other people (and even in places) as you read and take notes.

contd

DON'T FORGET

At this point, decide how you are going to organise your study file for *The Strange Case of Dr Jekyll and Mr Hyde*. Are you going to keep notes chapter by chapter, noting key events, character information and themes as they emerge? Experiment during the first chapters to see what works best for you.

CAN YOU EXPLAIN?

Until this chapter, we have had to rely largely on Utterson for an answer to the question: what exactly is the truth about the respectable Doctor Jekyll and his strange friend Edward Hyde? Utterson often struggles to make sense of what he has seen or fails to interpret events correctly. But now, we get the 'full statement' of the facts, from the man most concerned, Dr Jekyll himself. Incidents and situations which had puzzled Utterson – and indeed some readers – now find their explanation from Jekyll's own testimony. From this chapter, we can now find satisfactory answers to the following questions:

1   Why did Jekyll leave a will leaving all to Hyde?

2   Why is Hyde younger and smaller than Jekyll?

3   Why does Hyde never dine at the doctor's?

4   Why is the murder of Carew carried out so savagely?

5   Why did a new life begin for Jekyll after the Carew murder?

6   Why did Jekyll slam down the window on Utterson and Enfield?

7   Why did Utterson and Poole find a broken key with the breaks in it rust covered?

8   Where is the body of Henry Jekyll?

ONLINE

Check your answers on
www.brightredbooks.net

THINGS TO DO AND THINK ABOUT

Motifs are ideas or images which help support the guiding themes of the novel in which they appear. This novella is particularly rich in motifs. Here are a few of the more obvious. Try to comment on their usefulness in this particular story. Can you connect them with major themes in the novel?

Doors	
Locks, safes and barred windows	
Fog, weather and night	
Connecting buildings	

ONLINE TEST

Visit the Bright Red Digital
Zone to test your knowledge!

ROBERT LOUIS STEVENSON: GETTING TO GRIPS WITH THE TEXT

LET'S TRY THAT OUT

Poole swung the axe over his shoulder; the blow shook the building, and the red baize door leaped against the lock and hinges. A dismal screech, as of mere animal terror, rang from the cabinet. Up went the axe again, and again the panels crashed and the frame bounded; four times the blow fell; but the wood was tough and the fittings were of excellent workmanship; and it was not until the fifth that the lock burst asunder, and the wreck of the door fell inwards on the carpet.

The besiegers, appalled by their own riot and the stillness that had succeeded, stood back a little and peered in. There lay the cabinet before their eyes in the quiet lamplight, a good fire glowing and chattering on the hearth, the kettle singing its thin strain, a drawer or two open, papers neatly set forth on the business table, and nearer the fire, the things laid out for tea; the quietest room, you would have said, and, but for the glazed presses full of chemicals, the most commonplace that night in London.

Right in the midst there lay the body of a man sorely contorted and still twitching. They drew near on tiptoe, turned it on its back, and beheld the face of Edward Hyde. He was dressed in clothes far too large for him, clothes of the doctor's bigness; the cords of his face still moved with a semblance of life, but life was quite gone; and by the crushed phial in the hand and the strong smell of kernels that hung upon the air, Utterson knew that he was looking on the body of a self-destroyer.

'We have come too late,' he said sternly, 'whether to save or punish. Hyde is gone to his account; and it only remains for us to find the body of your master.'

The far greater proportion of the building was occupied by the theatre, which filled almost the whole ground storey, and was lighted from above, and by the cabinet, which formed an upper storey at one end and looked upon the court. A corridor joined the theatre to the door on the by street; and with this, the cabinet communicated separately by a second flight of stairs. There were besides a few dark closets and a spacious cellar. All these they now thoroughly examined. Each closet needed but a glance, for they were all empty and all, by the dust that fell from their doors, had stood long unopened. The cellar, indeed, was filled with crazy lumber, mostly dating from the times of the surgeon who was Jekyll's predecessor; but even as they opened the door, they were advertised of the uselessness of further search by the perfect mat of cobweb which had for years sealed up the entrance. Nowhere was there any trace of Henry Jekyll, dead or alive.

Poole stamped on the flags of the corridor. 'He must be buried here,' he said, hearkening to the sound.

'Or he may have fled,' said Utterson, and he turned to examine the door in the by street. It was locked; and lying nearby on the flags, they found the key, already stained with rust.

'This does not look like use,' observed the lawyer.

'Use!' echoed Poole. 'Do you not see, sir, it is broken? much as if a man had stamped on it.'

'Ah,' continued Utterson, 'and the fractures, too, are rusty.' The two men looked at each other with a scare.

'This is beyond me, Poole,' said the lawyer. 'Let us go back to the cabinet.'

They mounted the stair in silence, and still, with an occasional awestruck glance at the dead body, proceeded more thoroughly to examine the contents of the cabinet. At one table, there were traces of chemical work, various measured heaps of some white salt being laid on glass saucers, as though for an experiment in which the unhappy man had been prevented.

'That is the same drug that I was always bringing him' said Poole; and even as he spoke, the kettle with a startling noise boiled over.

QUESTIONS

1 Using your own words as far as possible summarise what happens in this extract. You should make at least four key points.   **4**

2 Look at the first paragraph.
   (a) Show how one example of the writer's use of language conveys Poole's strength in breaking down the door.   **2**
   (b) Show how one example of the writer's use of sentence structure suggests the difficulty he encountered in breaking the door down.   **2**

3 Look at paragraph three.
   By referring to an example of the writer's language explain how the writer effectively conveys the room's normality.   **2**

4 By using your own words as far as possible, explain why searching the cupboard and cellar spaces was a pointless exercise in the search for Jekyll.   **2**

5 By referring to this extract and to elsewhere in the novel, show how the character of Utterson is developed.   **8**

Total marks 20

HINTS FOR ANSWERS

Question 1

Any one for one mark. Possible answers include:
- Poole attacks and eventually breaks down the door to Jekyll's study.
- They find a normal teatime scene.
- They also find Hyde's dead body.
- Wondering where Jekyll is, they set out to look for him in the laboratory block.
- They look in all the nooks and crannies of this building.
- Everything looks dusty and cobwebby as if it hadn't been used for years.
- Poole suspects Jekyll is buried beneath the floor.
- They find a broken rusty key.
- As they look among Jekyll's chemicals, the kettle boils over.

Question 2

(a) Comment (×1) and reference (×1) for 2 marks.

Word choice: *blow shook the building:* the fact that the building moved shows the force he applied.

red baize door leaped: he managed to make some dramatic impact on this door despite its resistance.

panels crashed: he was able to destroy the panels of this stout door.

frame bounded: the fact that the wood round the door jumped suggests his force was such that it moved than the door itself.

(b) Comment (×1) and reference (×1) for 2 marks.

Repetition: *up went the axe <u>again, and again</u> the panels crashed...*

Lists attempts*: four times the blow fell...not until the fifth*

Long complex sentence made up of multiple clauses suggesting the problematic, lengthy nature of getting through the door.

Question 3

Comment (×1) and reference (×1) for 2 marks.

quiet lamplight: the dim light gave a peaceful glow.

a good fire glowing [and chattering]: the fire gave a cosy atmosphere to the room.

the kettle singing: tea-making was clearly in the air, as in a normal household.

papers neatly set forth: there appeared to be nothing disturbing the tidy desk, all was business-like.

things laid out for tea: tea being anticipated suggested all was normal.

Question 4

The doors of the cupboards they looked in were so dust covered, it was clear they hadn't been used for years (1) the cellar entrances were so covered in spiders' webs that they blocked anyone going in. (1)

Question 5

Utterson is someone given to observing carefully but not understanding the implications of what he is seeing or jumping to false conclusions. (1) Earlier, observing Hyde was the chief beneficiary of Jekyll's will, he assumes, wrongly, that Jekyll is being blackmailed. (1) *the ghost of some old sin, the cancer of some concealed disgrace, punishment coming years after.* (1) *...it only remains for us to find the body of your master.'(1)* he says here, never even considering for a moment that this body might in fact be Jekyll. (1) Earlier, when seeing a similarity in handwriting between a dinner invitation of Jekyll's and a letter said to be written by Hyde, he jumps to the conclusion that Jekyll is covering up for Hyde. (1) *'What!'* he thought. *'Henry Jekyll forge for a murderer!'* (1) Similarly, he fails to understand fully the extent of Dr Lanyon's horror at Jekyll's research, dismissing it casually with *'They have only differed on some point of science,'* he thought... (1)

PORTFOLIO

BETTER PORTFOLIO WRITING

By this stage in your studies, you are no stranger to essay-writing of all kinds. But, for National 5, you will need to ensure your writing has that added sparkle to maximise your final grade. So, how do you do that?

READ AROUND

The surest way to improve your writing style is to familiarise yourself with quality writing of all kinds: novels, short stories, biographies, travel writing and quality journalism are just a few genres to explore. By all means read for the pleasure they offer, but now is the moment to read quality texts with an added purpose: <u>to see what you can learn from professional writers</u>.

The gripping start to a story, the bringing to life of a character or setting, dialogue that crackles with realism: all these can profitably be studied for the improvement of your creative and reflective writing. The engagingly witty opening to an informative article, the usefulness of illustrative examples, the seamless transition from one paragraph to another: these are all aspects of quality journalism you can absorb to add persuasive conviction to your discursive texts. There is no shortage of models out there to study. Adopt a few ideas from the professionals, adapt them to suit your purpose – and you'll quickly see how your writing will progress!

WHAT DO I ALREADY KNOW?

Another way to raise your standards – one that's been right under your nose for some time – is to think about all the technical features you've been noting as you analyse RUAE texts. So, how about bringing some of them into your own writing?

You're used to explaining the impact of minor sentences, inversion, metaphors, word choice, parallel structures to name only a few, so how about making all this hard-won information work for *you* in another context? We'll spend some time looking at this approach – but, before you even switch on the computer, you would do well to spend some time thinking over these practical considerations to get top grades.

TIPS FOR TOP GRADES

- **Does it interest me?** Do not even think about committing yourself to paper until you are sure what you are writing about is something that truly interests you. Whether it's a short story about a friendship that went wrong or an analysis of the future of renewable energy sources, spend plenty of time considering whether the core idea *really* interests you. Are you willing to spend many hours on this topic? If in doubt, the chances are it's the wrong choice. It will save a lot of time and effort in the long run if you do some hard thinking before you start.

- **Do I know about it?** Write from your existing knowledge base or about a topic you want to get to know about. If you don't know about deserted tropical islands, it's clearly not the setting for your short story – unless you want to do some serious research. Discursive writing will always need research. Are you sure how to get the most reliable, up-to-date information? And are you interested enough in the topic to *want* to set about getting it?

- **Do I have a plan?** Before even drafting a word, plan your ideas in rough. Use whatever method works for you: a mind-map, a listing of possibilities, a page of random brainstorming thoughts. Mull over them all, eventually discarding the non-starters before trying to organise the remaining ones into some rough outline of paragraph content and sequence.

- **Have I considered my audience?** You are not yet a professional writer writing exclusively to please yourself. Yes, of course you should enjoy your own writing, but remember you are also writing to impress examiners in a public exam. So, try to keep that in mind at all times. Crisp, clear prose which hangs together well and which offers a rich reading experience is what they are looking for. Indulge them.

- **Have I considered my purpose?** What are you setting out to do? Entertain? Persuade? Analyse? Whatever your ultimate aim, you need at all times to be examining your language to see if it is fulfilling the purpose you think it is. It is easy to set out on a persuasive tack and then discover that your language later on has become simply factual and informative. Keep checking that you are using the language appropriate for the task you have set yourself.

- **Is my plan working?** Yes, we all need a plan to get started, but, as your text progresses, are you noticing weaknesses or possibilities you didn't at first consider? Relax. It's a good sign, showing that you're beginning to think like a professional writer. Don't be scared to move paragraphs about, delete sentences, add phrases, discard a word to find a better one or whatever now seems necessary. With information technology, all this becomes relatively easy.

- **Is this the best I can do?** Don't get so lost in your story or analysis that you forget to check basic essentials. Before handing in any draft, make sure you proofread it to check the grammar, spelling, punctuation and vocabulary. Don't be caught out by basics like *its/it's, their/there, to/too* and so on. Mistakes like these indicate a lack of respect towards your own text – and towards the examiner, too.

ONLINE TEST

Check if your idea for your portfolio-writing piece ticks all the boxes online at www. brightredbooks.net/N5English

THINGS TO DO AND THINK ABOUT

The portfolio is the ideal place for people who feel that exams do not bring out the best in them. Here they can really show what they can do. So, consider portfolio choices carefully. This is where you can really bring up your grade. Think back over the kind of writing you have excelled in. Don't be in a hurry to decide on a topic or genre. Study the tips above as you try out a few ideas before settling on any one. Show results to friends to see how they react. It's not just any piece of writing; it's the most important piece you've tackled so far. Make it work for you.

WHAT DO I HAVE TO WRITE?

You are expected to write two portfolio pieces of 1000 words each, which will account for 30% of your final grade. For people who are not always at their best in exams, this is a chance to make a major difference to your grade. For with portfolio work, you have time to consider what you want to write, time to write it and, most important of all, time to edit it carefully to ensure that these two pieces show your writing skills at their very best.

WHAT ARE MY CHOICES?

One of your two pieces will be drawn from the genres identified in Group A, the other from Group B. The group possibilities are as follows:

Group A: Creative

- a personal essay or a reflective essay
- a piece of prose fiction (e.g. short story, episode from a novel)
- a poem or set of thematically linked poems
- a dramatic script (e.g. scene, monologue, sketch)

Group B: Discursive

- a piece of transactional writing
- a persuasive essay
- an argumentative essay
- a report for a specified purpose

Before making any decisions about your choices, let's take a look at two popular genres in each group to see what each one involves. That way, you'll have a better idea which ones best match up to your skills.

Group A: Creative

Prose fiction	Personal/reflective
If you are someone who has always enjoyed writing short stories or episodes from a novel, this is a really pleasurable choice. If you are not already sure if this is something you enjoy, a portfolio piece for an important exam probably isn't the best place to find out.	Nobody can write better about you, your life and your reflections than you yourself. You already have all the information to hand, it's just a question of digging deep to bring the experience alive for others.
Opportunities Within the word limit, you are free to create your own world: atmospheric settings, characters who become convincingly alive, dialogue that fully reflects the characters and their lifestyles. Their fates are all in your gift. You must be prepared to explore all the possibilities of figurative language in the way of a professional writer.	**Opportunities** In personal or reflective writing you need to offer readers the same rich reading experience as you would in a short story. The difference is that in personal writing you are not creating an imaginary event or experience but considering one which you have lived through yourself. In reflective writing, you are considering aspects of the world around you which has captured your attention or imagination.
Considerations A successful piece of short fiction needs a strong sense of structure, it cannot just ramble on. You will find the word limit imposes restrictions on any unnecessary material. Here a plan is very necessary before you begin. Feel free to alter it, but never lose sight of the overall shape. Limit your characters if they are to be described fully. Remember that contrasting characters will spark conflict which is great for moving stories on.	**Considerations** Whether it's a personal or a reflective essay, make sure the topic has sufficient depth to sustain your interest – and your reader's – for a whole essay. As in a short story, your language should draw on many of the techniques you have been studying in your RUAE work: sentence structure, word choice, repetition etc. are just some of the ways you can enliven your text.

Group B: Discursive

Argumentative and persuasive writing

Here you have an opportunity to demonstrate your grasp of issues which affect us all. Learning how to research a topic, how to organise your findings convincingly and how to present them with authority will be invaluable not only in this exam but in other subjects – and in your life beyond school or college.

Argumentative writing

Opportunities

In this genre, you lay out factually and neutrally two sides of a topic in a logically organised structure. You may already know of a topic which you would enjoy examining in more detail. If not, quality journalism will alert you to the 'hot' topics of the day. The essential is to enjoy researching and sharing your results in prose which reads fluently and carries real conviction.

Considerations

Objective tone is of key importance in argumentative writing. Remember, too, the best discursive writing needs research to convince, but facts and expert opinion are only a starting point; you need to organise your own clear line of argument throughout.

Persuasive writing

Opportunities

Here, objective tone is thrown to the winds. You are an advocate for a subject/issue about which you feel strongly, so you need to work on persuasive tone throughout. (Check out the features of persuasive tone on page 29) You should adopt an outgoing, unashamedly emotive approach.

Considerations

While your tone needs to be persuasive, it should not become an empty rant. Remember to include up-to-date, well-researched information as well as emotive appeals. Check, too, that your persuasive tone is sustained throughout and not just in the opening paragraphs.

 ONLINE

For some advice about writing short stories, visit 'Your Story Club: How to write short stories – 10 tips with examples by our chief editor' at www.brightredbooks.net/N5English

 ONLINE TEST

Check if you have chosen the best writing option online at www.brightredbooks.net/N5English

 DON'T FORGET

Don't finally commit yourself to any essay choice until you are sure you know enough about the topic or are really keen to learn about it.

 DON'T FORGET

Start to try out ideas and plans well before the deadline; be prepared to accept that your first thoughts might not be your best ones. Successful portfolio-writing is about being willing to draft and redraft several times before you even think of presenting a first version to your teacher.

 THINGS TO DO AND THINK ABOUT

Reflect carefully before choosing. Notice that we have not looked at all the genres you might explore in your portfolio. Remember, however, that the writing of poetry and plays is a highly specialised art. Perhaps you have experience of writing in these genres and have had your work noticed by experts in these fields. If this is the case, then these might be choices worth considering. There is useful help to be had by consulting the poetry and drama pages in our 'Critical Reading' section. For most candidates, however, the possibilities we have looked at above are probably the most accessible and offer choices with which you will perhaps feel most comfortable – and which offer you the surest chances of success.

WRITING CREATIVELY

ONLINE

Use this online guide to the elements in a short story for extra help in getting started: 'Short story elements' at www.brightredbooks.net/N5English

WRITING PROSE FICTION

Short story or episode from a novel? An intriguing choice – but, whichever you choose, remember that <u>character</u> and <u>setting</u> are as important as <u>plot</u> in both. Characters that do not come alive, who simply remain names on a page, fail to engage the reader's interest; narratives that take place in a vacuum create little in the way of atmosphere to catch the reader's attention. Remember, too, that your word limit is only 1000 words. That means you have to set certain limitations on your narrative. Keep this in mind when you set about your planning.

So, how do you go about planning your prose fiction?

One way is to set yourself a number of 'wh-' tasks which you can tackle in any order you wish, depending on how you like to compose fiction. Do you prefer starting with setting, characters or plot? Here are some starting points.

Where?	• Setting is a key factor in a good short story. A detailed, realistic setting is a grand start to a fiction piece. But don't do it well in the first paragraphs and then forget all about it. Keep it going with brief references to it as the story progresses.
	• To write well about setting, you need to know it intimately. Write from your knowledge, either first-hand or from research.
	• Given your word limit, restrict changing setting too often. You will use up too many words.
	• Think of films you have enjoyed where the setting transported you to somewhere that felt totally real. Your narrative should do the same.
Who?	• Your word limit means you would do well to restrict your characters to a number you can describe adequately. Don't introduce characters who play little part in the final outcome. Two, three or four might be a sensible cast list.
	• Contrasting characters often lead to conflict, which moves a story along very nicely. For example, try contrasting youth and age, rich and poor, sensible and rash, shy and outspoken or good-natured and quick-tempered.
	• Jot down facts about each character before you start. Not just appearance, but personality traits, nervous habits, likes, dislikes, hobbies, interests, tastes in music, people, food and so on. Don't blurt these all out at once, but weave them from time to time into your narrative. Passing references to such features bring characters alive.
What?	• Again, your word limit reduces the kind of story you can handle here. Epic adventures are out. To be successful, a good short narrative need not be about dramatic events; a minor incident carefully observed and imaginatively related is more likely to suit the required length of your text. Time sequences of hours, days or weeks are probably more practical than years or decades as your time frame.
When?	• The present causes less trouble, but if you have an interest in earlier periods, some basic research might furnish a credibly different setting, while a fertile imagination could provide the detail necessary to convince in a sci-fi tale.
	• Remember that setting encompasses not only a place and period but the seasons, weather and time of day as well. These can be manipulated tellingly to bring atmospheric colour to your fiction. Use them to reflect changing moods and attitudes of your characters in their situations. For example, spring/green shoots/hope or evening/mist/threat.
Why?	• Credibility is something you need to be alert to. So, why something happens needs to be addressed carefully. The far-fetched can weaken even the most carefully realised settings and characters. Keep the plot within the bounds of the believable.
How?	• As important as the 'wh-' questions is the question of how the story is to be told. Is the narrator to be 'I'? This will bring you close to the speaker and his/her thoughts. Or are you going to use the third-person narrator: he or she? This will let you observe everyone and allow you into everyone's thought processes.
	• And how is the plot to advance? In normal time sequence or by a dramatic flash-forward or flash-back? These latter two will get you off to a flying start before you go back and fill in the details. Many successful films use this technique.

A USEFUL STRUCTURE FOR A PLOT

Some guides to writing short stories will tell you that the following is a useful structure:

- a settled situation involving a minimum of characters (perhaps two or three)

- a complication deriving from something happening: a letter arriving, an accident, a new character appearing, the loss of someone or something

- an increase in tension due to the new situation

- a crisis leading to a turning point in the affairs of all concerned

- an ending with a perceived change in matters compared with how they stood at the start. Perhaps the unhappy are now happier, perhaps a relationship has altered – for the better or the worse, or perhaps characters simply have changed their view on themselves or someone else. Or perhaps we readers have changed our perception of a character or situation.

You can probably think of many good short stories which use only some of these features or perhaps none at all. But, if you are stuck for a structure, this might be a useful starting point.

THINGS TO DO AND THINK ABOUT

Writing well means reading widely. Reading as many short stories as you can will give you ideas in all kinds of ways. You may already have looked at some in class.

As a starting point, you might try looking out for the *Oxford Book of Scottish Short Stories* or the *Oxford Book of Short Stories* in your library. They are both rich mines of short-story writing from which you can learn a lot. Look out for writers' use of metaphors, similes and symbols to see how they can give added impact to situations in your own writing.

 ONLINE TEST

Test the strength of your plot against this online checklist: www.brightredbooks.net/N5English

 DON'T FORGET

Of course, the best way to learn to write convincing short stories is to read as many of them as you can! Your school or college library will have no shortage of anthologies. Try looking out for the *Oxford Book of Scottish Short Stories* or the *Oxford Book of Short Stories*. They are both a rich mine of short-story writing from which you can learn a lot.

EXAMINING FICTION FOR WRITING TIPS

Early on in this section, we suggested that many of the techniques you learned about in RUAE or in analysing fiction could help you with your writing. How? Well, when analysing how writers make certain effects, you frequently point out the use of short or minor sentences, inversion, imagery, word choice and suchlike techniques. So, once you have decided on your plan, think carefully about how the story is to be told. Think about using the techniques employed by professional writers in a story you've enjoyed to do tasks such as launching a narrative, establishing a setting or creating a character.

LAUNCHING A NARRATIVE

Here is the beginning of 'A Chitterin Bite' by Anne Donovan. Look at the techniques employed to capture the reader's attention right from the very start. Many are familiar to you from your RUAE work.

Inversion of placing of names, catching conversational tone		Alliteration, for atmospheric description

> *We'd go tae the baths every Saturday morning, Agnes and me. Ah'd watch fae the windae, along the grey, gluthery street, till ah caught the first glimpse of her red raincoat and her blue pixie hat turnin the corner, then ah'd grab ma cossie, wrap it up in the blue-grey towel, washed too many times, and heid for the door.*
>
> *Ah'm away, Mammy.*

Adjectives of colour contrasting with the greyness of the environment

Washed-out colour of the worn towel suggesting relatively poor background

Long sentence, capturing the repeated ritual of Saturday mornings

Short sentence of simple direct speech after longer sentence, hinting at youth of speaker, also situating story in Scotland

Here, in only around 100 words, Anne Donovan has used some techniques with which you are familiar to do various things: to create, with great economy, a social setting for the two girls; to establish the fact of their ongoing friendship; to give an idea of their age. Nothing has been spelt out, but all the information is there. Note, too, Donovan's use of Scots for both narrative and dialogue, which further positions her characters. Scots for either narrative or dialogue might give an added sense of realism to your writing, too, depending on the situation you are creating.

LET'S LOOK AT THAT

Here is someone trying to use similar techniques to create a story of his own. Note there is no slavish attempt to mimic exactly Donovan's writing, but lessons have been learned.

Inversion of placing of names, catching conversational tone	*We were inseparable in those days, <u>Watty and me</u>. And the Monday-night routine was always the same: Watty would arrive on his <u>silver-sprayed sports</u> bike with the <u>Wonder-Woman transfers</u>, dump it any-old-how behind our straggly hedge, bang on the door since the bell had long since given up the ghost – and dad had never been a great DIY fan.*	**Alliteration to bring alive the garish quality of the bike**
Short burst of direct speech to contrast with this sentence and signal age, Scottish origin and sporting interests of speaker		**Long sentence to catch the routine nature of the Monday-night ritual and nature of family**
	Training's finishing late, dad. See ya.	

And here, as you can see, alertness to the techniques learned in analysing text can bring alive your own writing. Don't let your knowledge of inversion, the contrasting of long and short sentences, alliteration, imagery – and all the other techniques you have learned – remain shut away in your RUAE knowledge. You shouldn't follow a model from a professional writer slavishly, but be aware of possibilities. Apply aspects of them thoughtfully to your own writing where you think they will add interest. Experiment with them. They should make a difference to the colour and readability of what you write.

 ONLINE

Check out this advice about different ways to start a short story: 'The 7 Types of Short Story Opening' at www.brightredbooks.net/N5English

 ONLINE TEST

Test your knowledge of language techniques in this test: www.brightredbooks.net/N5English

 ## THINGS TO DO AND THINK ABOUT

Before you start out on a full-scale narrative, try out a few small-scale practice pieces to establish setting. It's a bit like a painter trying a few sketches before starting on a full-scale oil painting. Here are two brief situations which you might treat as the openings of a narrative.

Your task here is to create a convincing setting, using perhaps some of the following: onomatopoeia, imagery, alliteration, assonance, inversion or a variety of short and long sentences. Use any other techniques you think useful.

1 *It is a moonlit, frosty December night around ten o'clock. This character is entering a wooded area which he/she needs to cross to get home after a night out with friends. Bring the setting alive for the reader. Think of including the character's feelings if you can.*

2 *You wake up in a hotel room in some holiday destination, having arrived late at night. You have not seen much of the surroundings. The sun wakens you. You get up, open the blinds. Describe what you see and feel.*

How well did your writing go? Get a partner to underline any techniques he/she saw at work. Get their comment on how convincing your setting was. Do they have anything to add? This was just for practice – but, if it went well, could you develop one of these openings for the start of your real story?

 DON'T FORGET

Make your knowledge of the techniques you spot at work in analysing passages from journalism or fiction work for you when it comes to your own writing. You have a goldmine there. Profit from it.

 DON'T FORGET

Setting is something that needs to be kept refreshed. Don't establish it at the start and just let the rest of the story continue in a situational vacuum. Flowers wither; rain goes off; the sun goes in; changes happen. Record them. They all add to the atmosphere of the world you're creating and perhaps the mood of your characters.

CREATING CONVINCING CHARACTERS

THE SURFACE AND BENEATH

Happily, there is no single way of bringing characters alive on the page. Describing <u>appearance</u> is of course a start.

EXAMPLE:

Here is Ian Rankin describing Ludovic Lumsden in *Black & Blue*. Much of the detail goes into the description of his clothes; but, towards the end, lifestyle details creep in:

> Lumsden wore a blue blazer with shiny brass buttons, grey trousers, black slip-on shoes. His shirt was an elegant blue and white stripe, his tie salmon-pink. The clothes made him look like the secretary of some exclusive club, but the face and body told another story. He was six feet two, wiry, with cropped fair hair emphasising a widow's peak. His eyes weren't so much red-rimmed as chlorinated, the irises a piercing blue. No wedding ring. He could have been anywhere between thirty and forty years old. (p. 166)

Lumsden comes across as a smart dresser, but his obvious keenness for keeping fit is also suggested. He will turn out to be a corrupt policeman, but at the moment Rankin's depiction is neutral. Or is he just *too* smart to be true?

EXAMPLE:

Louise Welsh in 'The Cutting Room' adopts a very different approach to character presentation. Here the description is not in the objective third person but in a very subjective first-person narrative where we learn much more about Rilke, a Glasgow auctioneer, than simply his appearance:

> I'm twenty-five years at the auction house, forty-three years of age. They call me Rilke to my face, behind my back, the Cadaver, Corpse, Walking Dead. Aye, well, I may be gaunt of face and long of limb but I don't smell and I never expect anything. (p. 2)

Physical description is kept brief here (*gaunt of face and long of limb* – which, of course, we know from our RUAE work is an example of a parallel structure), but we also learn something of his <u>personality</u>: shrewdly knowledgeable about how he is viewed by others behind his back and yet chattily accepting of their nastiness (*Aye, well, I may be … but I don't smell and I never expect anything*).

Let's try that out

Using the approach adopted by Rankin and the approach adopted by Welsh, construct two descriptions of yourself as if you were a character in a short story. In the first, catch your physical appearance; in the second, try to hint at your personality, too. Go back and look at sentence structure in both, use of imagery, informal tone, narrative stance (third person and first person), parallel structures; try to incorporate what you think useful into your own writing here.

ONLINE

For more great character entrances, check out this article: '13 Great Movie Character Entrances' at www.brightredbooks.net/N5English

SHOW, DON'T TELL

Think about the entrance of Tybalt in the Baz Luhrmann film of *Romeo and Juliet*. He exits his car, grinding a cigarette butt under his metal heel in a way that suggests his cruelty and aggression long before he says anything. Think of other films where a small action can reveal much about character and mood: a flower placed carefully on a breakfast tray, a beer can crushed in a fist. Make small, giveaway actions part of your equipment for tackling character creation.

contd

Let's try that out

Thinking of how actions can establish character, work with a partner on inventing actions you could integrate into your narrative to signal in advance to readers the characters of the following people:

an impatient person, a generous person, a hostile person,
a nervous person, a person with something to hide

Now try to write a sentence or two on each one, integrating this selected action into the launch of their character.

EXAMPLE:

A clumsy person

> Entering in some haste, Jackson's left foot caught the cable of my desk-lamp, bringing it crashing to the floor at his feet. 'Sorry. This is always happening to me,' he said, looking up apologetically as he bent to pick up the smashed, smoking bulb.

Here we're shown, not told, that Jackson is clumsy. How much more effective is this than the comment: *Jackson is the clumsiest person I know*?

Could short extracts like this perhaps trigger ideas for a short story? How might the speaker react to Jackson here? Who precisely is Jackson, and why is he here? Short bursts of writing in this way can sometimes lead to unexpected bonuses. Try it.

YOU ARE WHAT YOU SPEAK

If actions can help to create characters, so too can speech habits. The type of <u>dialogue</u> you give to your characters can also spare you a lot of explanatory writing. Here your knowledge of sentence structure should help you a lot. Characters can come alive by the way they talk.

Let's try that out

In the grid below on the left, you will see a variety of speech habits at work. Match them with their character-type suggested by the column on the right.

It's a job where ... how shall I put it? ... Where you need, you know ... to be, well, just a bit ... a bit ... decisive. Mm ... Yes, quite ... decisive.	**BOSSY**
Fetch me the television guide. And bring my glasses. Not the old ones. And put the cat out since you're up. Hop to it, sunshine!	**INSECURE**
Does this really suit me? Am I maybe too old to be wearing rugby shirts? Is it not just a bit flash? Or am I just being a bit neurotic here? What do you think?	**BORING**
I've been secretary of this bowling club now for many more years than I care to remember, more years than you've been alive I'd say, but I've always enjoyed the work, the excitement of the tournaments, the many generations of bowlers who've come my way, grand folk, all of them.	**BRISK**
Now, then. Let's see. Jake, you alright taking the girls? I'll follow in the Range Rover. Shall we meet up in Carlisle? It'll take about an hour. Right. Off we go!	**VAGUE**

Here we see that vague people may tend to leave sentences incomplete or fragmented; bossy ones may fire off a series of commands; insecure ones perhaps favour a series of questions seeking reassurance; long-winded, boring people might go in for rather lengthy sentences; and brisk, dynamic ones may express themselves in a series of short sentences.

 ## THINGS TO DO AND THINK ABOUT

Appearance, actions, speech habits, mannerisms, taste in clothes, music, films, nervous tics: they all play their part in humanising your characters. And the features that make up their characters need to crop up throughout the tale, not be confined to some opening statements.

PERSONAL WRITING

Let's get one thing straight: personal writing is *not* creative writing. It needs, however, to present the reader with an experience that is just as rich and rewarding as reading a short story or novel. The difference is that the events and experiences described are true and taken from your own life.

The reflection which emerges derives from these events and experience. This reflection is there to demonstrate that you are capable of viewing biographical material in a way that presents you as a thoughtful person, one who sees significance in what has been experienced and perhaps learned.

ONLINE

Read this article about the best college applications in the USA, most of which come from everyday experiences in personal reflective writing: 'The *New York Times*: Some of the more mundane moments in life make great essays' at www. brightredbooks.net/N5English

BUT NOTHING EVER HAPPENS TO ME!

No, you probably haven't won an Olympic medal or been an *X-Factor* finalist, but successful personal writing doesn't really rely on news-making experiences of this kind. Success in personal reflective writing can stem from very ordinary everyday experiences or events which, when explored in some detail, reveal that there is a lot more to you and your life than you think. Here are just a few ways of exploring that life.

ME, MYSELF AND I

There are so many angles to your life that the problem might be knowing where to start. Asking yourself a series of questions might help you to sort out a starting point.

Who am I?

This might seem rather an obvious place to start, but think about it for a moment. You would first need to consider yourself in your own assessment, but how do your friends, family or teachers appear to regard you? Are you the person they think you are, or is there another 'you', one you would like them to see? Or is there another 'you' who you'd like to be? How do you intend to bridge this gap? Talking about incidents or conversations which illustrate these various viewpoints would occupy several sections, with a final section bringing together your verdict on how you view the way forward.

Examining yourself from yet another angle, you might wish to write about your present personality when compared with the person you used to be when younger. How have you changed? What brought about these changes? How do you feel about these changes? Exploring precise events or incidents that might have triggered these changes could be highly productive.

What do I do?

The way you pass your time when you are not committed to the educational process can be dissected in many different ways. Obviously, there are leisure activities and hobbies which help to make you the person you are. How you first became aware of this activity, your first reactions to it, key incidents along the way, how you have changed as a person or what you have gained or learned as a result of the exposure to it are just some of the things that might be included.

For those with employment after or before school or college hours, the possibilities are equally rich in potential. A need for additional financial resources probably drove you to seek employment in the first place, but what were your feelings about this? What did

contd

you learn as you set about looking for work; how did you react to any upsets along the way? Working with other people poses certain challenges; were there episodes where you learned that the workplace can be very different from your educational experience? Using key incidents, illustrate what you have experienced, gained or learned about yourself, people and life generally.

Who do I care about?

Relationships of all kinds are central to everyone's life. And relationships change as time passes. Families break up and reform in other ways. Weddings and funerals affect us with many different, sometimes conflicting, emotions. Relationships within families alter as we grow up and develop. The same is equally true of solid friendships formed in early years, which we see changing as the years pass. Are there key moments or incidents which brought about these alterations? Describing these key incidents or events and exploring your feelings as they occurred can help you to come to terms with them. And comparing them with your feelings today is an exercise which offers rich pickings for personal reflective work.

What have I learned?

As we grow and develop, life can deal us all kinds of knocks and bruises. All experience, however, is surely useful for what it teaches us about ourselves and life in general. Failure can sometimes be more instructive than success. Examining disappointment can be a really therapeutic and constructive activity. On the other hand, sometimes we are taught about life without any painful experience at all, through encountering people who have inspired us or taught us a lot about life without setting out to do so. Watching a friend or family member deal with a difficult situation might teach us about courage, determination or loyalty. The incidents and people from whom we learn offer material to describe and reflect on in depth.

THINGS TO DO AND THINK ABOUT

With a partner or in a group, look at the questions above from the viewpoint of your own experience and extract two or three possibilities which might form the starting point for an essay of this kind. Discuss frankly with the group what you might include, and see how others respond to your choices.

ONLINE TEST

Test your idea for a personal reflective piece against this checklist online: www.brightredpublishing.net/N5English

DON'T FORGET

A politician once commented:

I was brought up to believe that how I saw myself was more important than how others saw me.

Robert Burns rather turned this on its head when he said:

> *O, wad some Power the giftie gie us To see oursels as others see us!*

Irrespective which of these remarks you believe to be more in tune with your thinking, keep both in mind as you write. Reflection on how you see yourself and how others may be viewing you will only add depth and breadth to your material.

REFLECTIVE WRITING

Like a personal essay, a reflective essay is centred on you. In a reflective essay, however, the focus is more on what passes through your mind rather than on what you do or have done in your life. You aim is to give pleasure and interest to the reader. Although information and events will obviously come into your text, giving information and narrating events is not what a reflective essay is all about. True, your essay might be triggered by a person, place or object, a relationship, a mood, a memory, a photograph. Or maybe it is sparked by a feeling, an idea or a belief. *But it is your reflection on them that is important.*

THE NATURE OF REFLECTION

What might be some of the features of an interesting reflective essay? Here are some suggestions:

Anecdote/ observation	To get your reader interested in your reflections, you need to make clear how this topic came to your attention in the first place and why you think it to be significant. This can often be triggered by an event or incident – but be careful not to let this happening dominate your essay. *Walk into my little brother's bedroom at any time during the evening and you are bound to find him glued to his Facebook page. He is inordinately proud of the number of 'friends' he has accumulated since the start of the year. (And woe betide anyone who dares to 'unfriend' him.) But, last night, looking at his rapt face bent over his laptop, I began to wonder how healthy this heavy reliance on virtual friends is. Wouldn't he be better off adding to his real-world friends? Wouldn't we all?* This is the writer's opening on a reflective essay about his response to the influence of social media. The opening paragraph needs to be a 'hook' to attract your reader's interest. Work on it as carefully as you would on the start of a short story.
Character presentation	The pronoun 'I' will be important here since it is your reflections and reactions that take centre stage in this essay. The presentation of yourself needs to be as carefully considered as that of any character in a short story. For people to be interested in and perhaps convinced by your reflections, you need to present yourself as someone balanced in your thinking, open to the ideas and reactions of others. Their views and your reactions to them are also fruitful areas to explore as your essay advances. *Now take my sister. She takes quite the opposite view, finding social media a means of making friends with people all over the world. In fact, she believes that...*
Language choices	Here, too, is another way in which your character will emerge. Remember that it is more attractive to talk *to* and not *at* the reader. Informal tone often works in this kind of essay, as though you were exchanging your thoughts with a friend. (See page 28 for features of informal tone.) Metaphors and similes will also help enrich the texture of your views, just as they would in a short story.
Process	Although you are sharing your thoughts with your reader, these cannot be presented as a loose collection of ideas; you need some kind of structure to shape your thought process. Your engagement with the topic might pass through several moods in the course of the piece. The overall tone might be *confiding* as you take people into your private thoughts about social media. It may become *exasperated* as you consider some aspect which you find unacceptable (e.g. how much more productive when time spent on real-world activities.) It may then move into *concerned* as you consider the risks young people face talking to complete strangers. It might be *amused* at the importance some people place on reporting the most trivial of events or happenings. By the end of the essay, your reflections may have passed through several of these moods. Make sure you signal changes of direction clearly to ensure the overall structural unity of your reflections.

ONLINE TEST ✓

Check how well you did online by filling in this quiz about the nature of reflection: www.brightredbooks.net/N5English

DON'T FORGET

A reflective essay, while it may employ some language features of a persuasive essay, does not set out to persuade readers of your points of view; it merely shares them.

POSSIBLE PATHS OF REFLECTION

Let's take a possible question to see how we might break it down for an essay. Not all topics might suit this approach, but it might be a useful starting point which you could possibly adapt to suit your own subject. The essential is to find the angles that you feel would be interesting to explore and to share with others.

EXAMPLE:

Have we all become slaves to the consumer society?

Topic introduced	Give a context/reason for your selection of this topic.	*Take a walk any day of the week to your nearest shopping mall and what do you see? Hundreds of shoppers wandering the aisles, some of them...*
Writer's overall stance outlined	Make clear your viewpoint on the phenomenon you are starting to explore.	*Let me make my viewpoint quite clear. To me it seems reassuring that many people nowadays enjoy a standard of living which allows them to turn their desires into reality, to brighten their routines with...*
Reflection aroused by topic	Flag up your concerns.	*This ongoing preoccupation with consumer goods, however, raises a number of questions. Has consumerism become our new religion? Are things becoming more important in our lives than...?*
Broader focus	How do others see this?	*Whatever my own misgivings, there is no doubting the growing popularity of shopping malls, Britain's new cathedrals of consumerism. Last year saw the opening of no less than... Some may see this as a healthy sign of democratic prosperity. Others view them as vital therapy for those who need... Others still might...*
Specific comment	Consider independent commentators.	*My mother, usually the thriftiest of people, sees a trip to our local mall as a high spot in her week... Writing in the Guardian no less a critic than xxxxx suggested that our consumer society...*
More comment	Consider involved participants.	*The number of shoppers waiting impatiently for malls to open seems only to increase...When interviewed, one actually said, '...' For another, her reason for being there was quite simply... Clearly, then, consumerism as symbolised by malls is...*
Summing up of view and final reflections	Pull various strands together.	*So what does this tell us about our society? Have we truly become slaves to consumerism? Perhaps it is a hopeful sign in that... But does it not also suggest that we are becoming... Is this phenomenon set to grow indefinitely or is it vulnerable to economic forces? As for me, come Saturday morning you'll find me...*

THINGS TO DO AND THINK ABOUT

Remember, it is the exploration of the topic which is important. You are not out to make the case for one side or the other or to persuade people to a certain point of view. Your role is to open up aspects of a topic that people may not have considered before and to share these thoughts with the reader.

ONLINE

For more tips on how to plan and execute a great piece of reflective writing, read this article: 'How to write an effective reflective essay' at www.brightredbooks.net/N5English

DON'T FORGET

A good reflective essay often takes the form of a mind making itself up before it comes to a conclusion. *Sometimes I feel that ... At other times, depending on my mood, I see things differently. Maybe, I think, I have been too ... My best friend Russell is no help at all. He believes that ... All things considered, however,*

WRITING DISCURSIVELY

In this group, you have a choice between writing an argumentative essay or a persuasive one. So, what are the differences?

- An argumentative essay is one in which you explore and evaluate opposing viewpoints on a controversial topic in formal and strictly neutral language, calling on objective data before offering any final opinion of your own.

- A persuasive essay is one in which you attempt to win over the reader to your view on a controversial topic. Here, too, there will be researched data to substantiate your viewpoint, but it will not be similarly balanced as in an argumentative essay. Contrary viewpoints may be entertained but only to be dismissed. Here the language will be unashamedly emotive as it seeks reader approval.

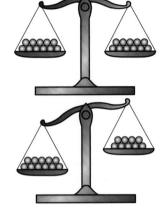

These are very different approaches to a topic, as you can see. But there are also likenesses, too, likenesses which it might be helpful to consider before making a final choice of one or the other.

ONLINE

If your topic reflects current issues and debates, the chances are that published texts may not have caught up with them fully yet. Quality journals and newspapers can help greatly here. Using a search engine, tap in your topic or issue followed by a quality online newspaper of your choice (the *Independent*, the *Guardian*, the *Herald*, the *Scotsman*, for example) to see what is available.

ARGUMENTATIVE AND PERSUASIVE: FAMILY LIKENESSES

Whichever approach you decide on, your completed essay must offer the reader just as much satisfaction on completion as any piece of fiction or reflective writing. So, how is this sense of satisfaction achieved? Let's answer this by asking some of the questions your reader might be asking of your argumentative or persuasive essay.

Why is this subject worthy of attention? In your introduction to an essay of either approach, you must establish enough background information to convince the reader that the topic is sufficiently important and compelling to be worth reading about, particularly if it is not currently in the news.

Is the writer respecting the genre? It would be foolish to set out to write an argumentative essay and then slip into personal views along the way, thus destroying your claim to objectivity. It would be similarly foolish for the writer of a persuasive essay to end up simply presenting information rather than seeking to persuade.

How reliable is the research? Your sources should be acknowledged at the end of your essay. So, how well will your list read? Nutritional 'facts' from the website of a fast-food manufacturer could hardly be taken to be evidence of sound research. Website information might be useful as a starting point for topics which have only recently touched our consciousness. So far, these may not have been dealt with in book form, but more traditional topics will have been explored in peer-reviewed publications. These are usually the most reliable and authoritative. Quality journals and newspapers employ acknowledged experts and pollsters whose accuracy and readability can usually be counted on. These, of course, can be viewed online, mostly free of charge. A list of sources balanced between the paper-based and the electronic will impress.

How up-to-date is the information? In this multimedia age of 24-hour newsgathering, there is no excuse for outdated statistics and information. Check publication dates of books, journals and newspapers and posting dates of websites before beginning note-taking.

Have sections been plagiarised? Research means note-taking. While engaged in this, ensure that you do not 'lift' unacknowledged stretches of text. Lifting text from websites or publications is simply theft, and experienced examiners have a sixth

contd

sense for detecting it. Often, this 'lifting' may have been accidental, but you must be alive to the danger. To avoid this, as you take notes, use a highlighter to differentiate quotations from your own notes, paying attention to the details of the author's name and status, place of publication and date of extract. Another way to avoid the dangers of inadvertent plagiarism is to put the idea straight into your own words, while, again, acknowledging whose idea this originally was.

THE NEED FOR AUTHORITY

Just as you need evidence in your Critical Essay, so, too, do you need it in discursive writing. Whether you decide on an argumentative essay or a persuasive one, you need evidence to support your case. In a critical essay, this took the form of close reference to the text or a quotation. Here it is the backing of what we call authority. By this, we mean the opinion of an acknowledged expert in their field, the results of a respected poll or a reference to a published study or report. In every instance, you need to make clear who your authority is, where and when the evidence appeared. Without authority, you are attempting to make out a case simply from your own subjective opinions. These, while no doubt interesting, will not carry the weight that expert opinion will. Having some expert evidence on both sides will immeasurably strengthen your arguments. But do not overuse this; it is only there to support *your* case.

THINGS TO DO AND THINK ABOUT

Argumentative and persuasive essays, for all their differences, share many characteristics. They both may contain:

- illustrative examples or anecdotes: to aid readers' understanding

- expert opinion: to support or criticise a point of view

- analogies: to suggest parallels with other situations to aid understanding

- polls or survey results: to demonstrate research-backed evidence

- warnings: to indicate ability to follow through implications of findings.

How they each use these shared features is, of course, very different, as we shall see later.

WRITING ARGUMENTATIVELY

LAUNCHING THE ARGUMENTATIVE STRUCTURE

In a successful argumentative essay, writers take a controversial topic and conduct in-depth research before presenting data to support both sides of the argument. Finally, if they so choose, they may award support to one viewpoint or the other. Balance of factual presentation and neutrality of language are the hallmarks of this form of essay.

The opening paragraph is particularly important for establishing your credentials as a reliable investigator of the topic. It needs to suggest that you are reliably informed, clear-sighted in your appraisal of the opposing viewpoints and well organised in your presentation of material. Let's see how an introduction for this kind of essay might work.

A topic that has aroused much controversy is fracking. This is a relatively new means of obtaining oil and gas which has environmentalists and businesspeople at loggerheads with each other. After studying the pros and cons of the topic, we might come up with the following format for the introduction:

Title in itself balances both viewpoints. Note the order in which they appear.	**Fracking: false prophet or real profit?**
Significance of topic established in first two sentences.	*The world is fast running out of polluting fossil fuels. Renewable sources of clean energy such as wind and solar power as yet seem some way from offering reliable alternatives. According*
Topic defined in third, fourth and fifth sentences	*to some experts, hydraulic fracturing, or fracking, is a plausible alternative to both. But what actually is it? Put simply, it is a process which extracts natural gas and oil from rock formations deep underground by fracturing and injecting chemicals into*
Sentence six sets out one side of argument – the negative.	*them. Opponents claim it is a dangerous tampering with nature, one which risks polluting water supplies and even causing earth tremors.*
Sentence seven sets out the positive viewpoint.	*Supporters claim it offers Britain a profitable source of secure energy which reduces exposure to international political*
Sentence eight suggests how the essay will develop (a) by examining the dangers and (b) by investigating the benefits. A road-map.	*upheavals. What exactly are the associated dangers, and how exactly could fracking help our environmentally-concerned world?*

Notice that in the title, in the setting out of the two arguments and in the final sentence, the positive is mentioned last, hinting perhaps on what side the essay will finally come down.

ORDERING YOUR ARGUMENTS

Like a critical essay, an argumentative essay should present a flow of ideas which carries readers comfortably along, with no sudden or unexplained changes of direction to jar or puzzle them. The sensible ordering of your ideas and arguments will strengthen your case-making skills immeasurably in the eyes of the examiner. So, how will you ensure this seamless flow of text?

One way would be to examine your evidence and then decide where your final verdict falls: are you for or against an idea? Suppose you decided you were *for* fracking as discussed earlier. Then you might usefully consider the following order of presentation:

- an introduction which sets out both sides but places the positive second
- subsequent paragraphs/sections which deal with the hazards of fracking
- leading to paragraphs/section looking at fracking's benefits
- a summative conclusion making finally clear where you stand on fracking, i.e. in favour of it.

Why this particular order?

Well, suppose you were in favour of fracking but left discussing its dangers until the second half of your essay. Consider, then, the effect on your readers if, in the very next, concluding paragraph, you abruptly announced that you were in favour of a process that you had just been expertly criticising. This can puzzle and disconcert your readers: one minute you are pointing out the shortcomings of an issue, the next you are saying you are in favour of it.

If you are in favour of a topic, then banish a discussion of its negative points to earlier in the essay so that your positive case seamlessly precedes your positive conclusion. The reader will not have forgotten your negative points, but the positive ones will be fresher in his/her mind, and your approval of them will seem all the more understandable and logical.

The reverse also holds good: if you are against an issue, acknowledge its benefits first and then discuss its shortcomings so as to lead into a conclusion that follows naturally on from these shortcomings.

If you decide to withhold an opinion of your own, be careful how you do so. This is a perfectly legitimate position to take up, but make sure you give a reason: current lack of credible evidence, a rapidly changing situation, or perhaps ultimately a verdict will depend on the individual's political/social/cultural views. Make sure you have reasons for rejection of commitment to one side or the other. If you do not, you risk simply looking like a ditherer.

ONLINE TEST

Test your knowledge of what makes up a good argumentative essay online, at www.brightredbooks.net/N5English

ONLINE

Struggling for somewhere to start? See if any of the argumentative essay topics on this list inspire you: '50 argument essay topics' at www.brightredbooks.net/N5English

DON'T FORGET

When you are constructing a case in favour of an issue, begin with a point strong enough to gain credibility, then go on to a stronger one and then finish with your best one. In this way, your argument builds, getting stronger and more impressive as it advances.

THINGS TO DO AND THINK ABOUT

Are you perhaps unsure where you stand on an issue, even after you have conducted considerable research? Try this. Once you have collected your data, why not organise the points in 'for' and 'against' columns? Then try writing an introductory paragraph for *both* sides, in the style of our 'fracking' introduction. Which version are you more comfortable with? That may give you the pointer you are looking for.

WRITING PERSUASIVELY

THE LANGUAGE OF PERSUASION

This is a form of writing which responds well to strong opinions. These opinions need, however, to be credibly supported by researched data, otherwise your essay will sound like an empty rant. There are plenty of models out there for you to study. Try first of all looking in the 'Opinion', 'Comment' or 'Leader' pages of a quality newspaper. Or listen to a politician making a speech in parliament. Here you'll find plenty of tips for writing (and speaking) persuasively. You'll notice that authority is often cited but skilfully manipulated to back up personal points of view. So, what would you do well to consider including? Let's take a look at some possibilities.

Involvement of reader

The use of pronouns such as 'we' and 'you' see you absorbing the reader into your arguments. 'We suffer here from too much bureaucracy ...' Commands also bring the reader closer. 'Consider for a moment ...', 'Think how much better ...'

Emotive language

Emotionally loaded word choice will feature prominently, as it does in much media reporting. 'Families' may become 'hard-working families'; 'pensioners' may become 'cash-strapped pensioners'; a pregnant woman may become 'a heavily pregnant woman'. The aim is to arouse sympathy/support for or anger/criticism against people and issues in your chosen sphere of persuasive writing. If you cite authority figures, they will often have emotive phrases attached to their names: 'Was it not Sir Walter Scott, Scotland's greatest novelist, who claimed that ...?', or 'To quote the much-maligned Tim Henman: ...'

Rhetorical questions

These questions, to which no real answer is expected of the reader, figure prominently in articles, speeches and persuasive essays. (They may, however, sometimes be answered by writers themselves, for effect, to demonstrate their clever mastery of a seemingly difficult problem which he/she has brought to our attention.) The aim of their authors is to seek our support by appealing to our feelings. 'What kind of parent treats children in this way?' 'When will governments learn there is no support for such policies?' Used occasionally, particularly after a stretch of information in which emotive word choice has been well to the fore, the effect can be powerfully persuasive. Used too often, they tend to sound rather hollow.

Attitude markers

After some particularly informative yet emotive reporting of information, these can be useful in guiding reader response. 'Clearly then, ...', 'Obviously, ...', 'Surely, ...', 'Sadly, ...', 'Fortunately, ...' are just a few. Look out for opportunities to use them to win over readers to your committed stance.

Rising rhetorical triads

Don't be put off by their name. You have heard them many times in speeches you may have listened to. They figure prominently in writing that is meant to persuade. They are closely related to the persuasive devices of **repetition** and **parallel structures** about which you learned in RUAE work. These tripartite statements or phrases typically appear in the final section or paragraph, with each element gaining in strength as the writer seeks to build to a <u>climax</u>. 'This is a tramway system which will ... It is a system which will also ... It is a system which, above all, will ...' Often they combine with rhetorical questions for even greater emotional impact. 'Is this the world we worked for? Is this the world we fought for? And is this a world worth passing on to our children?' Such a ringing close can work well in a persuasive essay, appealing as it does to the reader's emotional response. It will only work, however, if there is some solidly researched data elsewhere in the essay on which you can build such a final emotional pitch.

ONLINE

For more inspiration, check out the *Telegraph's* list of the 'Top 25 political speeches of all time' at www.brightredbooks.net/N5English

DON'T FORGET

The novelist Joseph Conrad once remarked:

'He who wants to persuade should put his trust not in the right argument, but in the right word. The power of sound has always been greater than the power of sense.'

With a partner or in a group, discuss whether you agree with Conrad. Do you see any dangers in this belief for you as a persuasive essay-writer?

ORDERING YOUR ARGUMENTS

In a persuasive essay, you are setting out to persuade readers of the rightness of your case. This frees you from the need to balance your arguments or present your case in language as neutral as in an argumentative essay. Here you are at liberty to use persuasive language techniques of the kind we have just been discussing.

You must be careful, however, to marshal your arguments just as carefully as in an argumentative essay, although somewhat differently. To win over readers, it is wise to establish yourself as a sensible, reasonable person. And sensible, reasonable people are always aware that their opinion is not the only one around. How, then, do you deal with possibly contrary viewpoints when you set out to make your own persuasive case? As in an argumentative essay, it might be wise to deal with them early on in your essay so that your increasingly powerful arguments push them aside in the memory of your readers.

This might be a possible solution:

- An introduction in which you make your viewpoint abundantly clear.

- Acknowledge perhaps a conflicting opinion but refute it in a reasonable, logical way. It is always a good idea to show respect to contrary views.

- Launch your first persuasive paragraph.

- Continue with similarly persuasive paragraphs, saving your strongest argument until last.

- Ringing conclusion.

THINGS TO DO AND THINK ABOUT

To get you started using persuasive techniques, consider the introductory paragraph for a persuasive essay entitled *Why we should all become organ/blood donors*. If you were writing the full essay, you would need to do some in-depth research, but a compelling introduction can be based on the topic's emotive appeal. Draft an introduction employing at least three of the persuasive features discussed here. Swap your introduction with a partner. Did they spot the persuasive devices you employed?

ONLINE TEST

Check if your plan fits the bill online at www.brightredbooks.net/N5English

WRITING PERSUASIVELY (contd)

LAUNCHING THE PERSUASIVE STRUCTURE

As in an argumentative essay, you need to quickly establish yourself as an informed commentator yet one, this time, with a firmly committed point of view. Let's take a look at how we might organise that introduction to create the best possible effect. Here we might go back to the topic of fracking which we dealt with in our argumentative introduction.

Note title is unashamedly persuasive, using alliteration and a command to add impact.	**Secure our future with fracking!**
First two sentences are questions which hook reader's attention by offering attractive propositions and also establish subject's significance.	*What would you say if we told you we were close to a source of fuel that was cheaper and potentially cleaner than oil and coal? What if we added that its extraction close to home would free us from the unpredictability of international politics? Hydraulic fracturing, or fracking, offers us hope on both fronts. But what*
Topic defined and explained in sentences three, four and five.	*actually is it? Put simply, it is a process which extracts natural gas and oil from rock formations deep underground by fracturing and injecting chemicals into them. Surely the time has come for all our*
Attitude marker launches final sentence (a rhetorical question) which both lists benefits and signals structure sequence of essay.	*politicians to get behind a process that offers enormous benefits to the environment, the economy and long-suffering consumers?*

The writer in the introduction here is highly enthusiastic about the benefits of fracking. This is not the only view, of course. In the 'Things to Do and Think About' section at the end of this topic, there is the chance to explore the other side of the argument more fully.

STRUCTURING THE PERSUASIVE PARAGRAPH

Notice that the paragraphs in a persuasive essay, just as in a critical, argumentative or creative essay, can benefit from what is by now a familiar structure: a strong statement (S) composed of one or more sentences to form the opening, followed by evidence (E) whose significance is unpacked for us in a commentary (C) of our own. Here are elements of a persuasive paragraph with that SEC structure:

For decades now, cosmetic surgery has bewitched yet bewildered women who feel their appearance falls far short of the image they crave. Research at the University of Geneva suggests that, in their desperate desire for change, women sometimes fail to make the most elementary of checks on ... (STATEMENT) According to Professor Erica Martin, writing in the August 2013 issue of ... (EVIDENCE) From disturbing statistics such as these, surely it is abundantly clear that Europe-wide legislation is urgently required if we are to eliminate such alarming risks to ... (COMMENTARY)

GIVING SOURCES FOR DISCURSIVE WRITING

Earlier in this section, we mentioned the importance of giving your sources for this kind of writing. Naturally, the more professionally you present the resources you have consulted, the more seriously your work will be taken. Bear in mind, too, when you go on to college or university, that setting your sources out correctly will be an important asset. There are several recognised ways of setting out sources. The following one is known as APA style (American Psychological Association) and is commonly used in British academic institutions.

contd

Referencing books

To reference books in the APA style:

> Start with author's name: surname first, then initial. (Followed by the year of publication in brackets) *Then comes the title in italics.* Then the city of publication: and finally the publisher.

A complete book reference should appear like this:

> King, R. (2000) *Brunelleschi's Dome.* London: Penguin.

Referencing newspapers and magazine articles

To reference articles from newspapers or magazines:

> Start with author's name: surname first, then initial. (Followed by the publication date in brackets) Next include the title of the article itself. *Then the name of the publication should come in italics.* And finally the page reference.

A complete article reference should appear like this:

> Goring, R. (2003, January 4) She's Talking Our Language Now. *Herald.* p. 14.

Electronically sourced material

To reference electronically sourced material:

Name of author (if available) and title of article/publication as you would for a print publication. In place of city of publication and name of publisher, put the web address and the date when the article was posted (if available) and also the date when you accessed.

ONLINE TEST

Check that your knowledge of paragraph structure and referencing is up to scratch online at www.brightredbooks.net/N5English

DON'T FORGET

All references should be arranged in alphabetical order. This should be by the first letter of the author's surname, or by the name of the website if there is no author listed!

ONLINE

For more information on listing web addresses, consult 'APA Lite for College Papers' at www.brightredbooks.net/N5English. See point 6.9 under Web Pages.

THINGS TO DO AND THINK ABOUT

As mentioned previously, there are numerous people against fracking (not least the artist of this cartoon!). Here are some points which opponents might put forward.

- Drilling activities have been known to cause earth tremors.

- Drilling can pollute aquifers (underground channels carrying water).

- Fracking requires great quantities of chemicals. These have to be transported to sites, creating additional pollution.

- In America, firms have not been quick to disclose how they dispose of these chemicals.

- If wells are not properly capped, harmful methane gas may escape, adding to greenhouse-gas worries.

- Increased traffic on roads is not welcome in small communities.

'Good news, George. Apparently our gas bills might be a few pence cheaper.'

Either with a partner or on your own, try to compose an introduction to a persuasive essay which is hostile to the idea of fracking. Obviously you will not have space to include all the contrary arguments; but select two key facts to weave into your introduction. First discuss which facts you think would be the most important to include. Give reasons for your final selection.

MANAGING YOUR PORTFOLIO

Writing can be a fairly lonely business. The need for concentration tends to make us want to shut ourselves away to get on with the task. Of course, you will maybe have discussed your choice of portfolio pieces with a friend or two and will have shown a plan to your teacher. But, once your plan has been approved, you will probably have set about your first draft in some quiet corner of the library or at home, perhaps showing the piece to somebody you know just before handing in the draft.

Now, friends being friends – and catching sight of your neatly typed manuscript – they will probably make polite noises. But what do they *really* think? Seeing clearly that your work is already far advanced, they probably won't tell you in any great critical detail. So, can we really call this peer-reviewing? Is it not more like going through the motions?

FIND A PORTFOLIO FRIEND!

A better method of working might be to find a 'portfolio friend' *right at the beginning* of the portfolio-planning process – somebody whose judgement you respect and who knows you and your work fairly well, somebody you see and talk to regularly.

Involve them right from the beginning of the process, not just at its end.

As you discuss possibilities, check with the relevant section of this Study Guide to see how it could help you with the various genres.

START WITH BASICS

Discuss together which genres for the portfolio you are each contemplating. Go through this Study Guide, looking at the kinds of writing which attract you and in which you may have already shown some ability. How difficult do you think you are going to find an argumentative essay at this level? If you went for that option, what might you choose to write about?

Maybe you like the idea of personal/reflective writing. Maybe you should revisit this territory. Bounce ideas off each other. List potential genres and discuss together the pros and cons of each one. Spend considerable time at this stage before even thinking of a specific title or topic, before planning or drafting a single word. Time well spent at this stage will probably save you a lot of time later on.

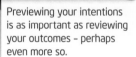

DON'T FORGET

Previewing your intentions is as important as reviewing your outcomes – perhaps even more so.

RESEARCH TOPICS TOGETHER

So, maybe you have decided on an argumentative essay and prose fiction. Let's look at them, one by one. Very well; so, what controversial topic are you interested in exploring? Discuss together what is involved in gathering evidence. How difficult or easy might this be, given the topic?

Is there any possibility that you could research a topic together, with your friend deciding on a persuasive essay and you an argumentative essay? By pooling your research, you would both become subject 'specialists', with your essays benefiting from the added depth and breadth of joint research.

Use this Study Guide's discursive section to help you try out some approaches to these kinds of writing. Does this kind of writing feel the right choice for you? What do you think? What does your partner think? Consult. Discuss. It's good to air your views, feelings and, yes, doubts at this early stage.

contd

Should you be considering a short story, a similar approach holds good. Is there an idea at the back of your mind? What does your partner make of it? A bit far-fetched? Too complicated for the word limits? Test out your ideas against the suggested processes in the prose section of this book.

TRIANGULATE ADVICE

Teachers have their roles to play in this process also. Once you have discussed your general intentions with your partner and your teacher, the time has probably come to shape up a plan for your teacher's inspection. Once you have the feedback, you are now in the healthy position of having a triple perspective on the plan.

CONSULT REGULARLY

Don't be in any hurry to complete the first draft. Your plan will have broken down the essay into several sections. Consult with your partner at each stage of creating these sections. If you were working on an argumentative essay, the process might go like this:

Introduction

After having checked what this Study Guide has to say about introductions, does your partner feel your introduction is appropriate? Parts missing? Too dull an opening sentence?

Body paragraphs

In a discursive essay, are they sufficient to explore fully your topic? How strong are the opening statements in each section? How convincing is the evidence you are producing? Does your commentary on the evidence do the evidence full justice?

Conclusion

Check again with this book to see if your conclusion matches up with what an examiner might expect. Does your partner agree with how you have rounded off your discussion of this topic? Are there any lingering weaknesses in his/her opinion?

Whatever genres you choose to explore for the portfolio, adopt a similar approach with your chosen partner for each of your two pieces. Remember, finally, that the examiners are looking for work that reveals appropriate:

- content
- structure
- expression
- technical accuracy

Make sure at this stage that each of these four criteria is being given sufficient attention. You will find that the interchange of ideas with your partner on all these points will strengthen not only your work but your self-confidence, too, as you proceed to the completion of the portfolio.

CONTINUE THE PROCESS

After your teacher has seen and made suggestions on how the draft might be improved, talk over the proposed changes with your partner. Redraft the local areas that need adjusting.

ONLINE

Check out the 'SQA Study Guides' at www. brightredbooks.net/N5English for more useful information on how to manage your time.

ONLINE TEST

Take the 'Managing your Portfolio' test online at www. brightredbooks.net/N5English

THINGS TO DO AND THINK ABOUT

In this electronic age, use e-mails to keep in touch with your partner. In this way, changes and improvements can be implemented more quickly and don't need to wait for a face-to-face encounter.

PROOFREADING YOUR PORTFOLIO

In the long process of preparing your drafts, you will likely have made numerous changes: perhaps a missing sentence was added, perhaps you inserted a quotation from a leading authority, or maybe you changed the order of certain paragraphs. This is all to the good. This is how a serious writing process should happen.

But there are hazards, too. As a result of all these improvements, irritating glitches may have crept in while you were concentrating on drafting the major changes. They may seem minor, but nevertheless they count against you in terms of technical accuracy. So, how do we avoid or eliminate them?

LEAVE TIME

Don't leave finalising your 'polished' draft to the last minute. If you allow yourself sufficient time, you can put your essay aside for some time before the due date and come back to it fresh for a final read-through. You will be astonished how many slip-ups you will notice straight away, slip-ups which totally escaped your notice in the white heat of drafting. So, here's another good reason for avoiding brinkmanship.

READ ALOUD

Here's where your portfolio friend can come in useful again. Reading a text through silently to yourself to check for errors can be unreliable. We tend to 'read' what we *think* we see rather than what is actually on the page. Better still, get your portfolio friend to read it back to you. He or she is more likely to read what is *actually* there rather than what *you think* is there.

Furthermore, hearing sentences read aloud can often help to detect clumsy expressions or sentences which either go on too long or do not quite make sense.

CHECK LINKAGE

A good essay, whether it be discursive, personal reflective or creative, needs to maintain a smooth flow from beginning to end. The introduction must flow into body paragraphs, and they in turn must run smoothly into each other before merging satisfyingly into your conclusion. Reading aloud will also help here. That clumsy, unprepared-for change of topic will immediately be obvious to the ear when read aloud, although it may have slipped by unnoticed on countless silent readings. There are the basics to demonstrate sequence such as:

Firstly, ...   *Furthermore, ...*   *In addition, ...*   *What is more, ...*   *Finally, ...*

These show simple progressions from one point in a sequence to the next one. But you may wish to use connectives of transition to move your reader from one topic to quite another:

Now, while it is true to say that ...   *As far as ... is concerned, ...*   *Turning to ...*
Regarding the question of ...

And, if you want to introduce a brief aside to your reader, there is always: *Incidentally, ...*

If you wish to make a change of direction from a preceding comment, you have various choices:

On the other hand, however, ...   *By way of contrast, there is ...*   *Conversely, ...*

SPELLCHECK

Yes, you've got a spellchecker on your computer, but there is only so much it can spot. It will help you out with the more difficult words, but it will not help you when you accidentally type 'bit' when you mean 'but'. Even in university dissertations, examiners constantly complain of finding the following very basic errors. Don't spoil fine work by confusing elementary items like these:

were/we're/where	who's/whose
too/to/two	they're/their/there
its/it's	lose/loose

Better still, go over *now* all the words you know you have been getting wrong in your essays for years. Get them right once and for all! You know which ones I mean!

CHECK PUNCTUATION

From your preparation for Close Reading, you should have a sound knowledge of how punctuation works in creating certain effects. Make sure you apply this knowledge to your own writing. Be particularly careful with direct speech in short stories or personal reflective writing.

WRONG: 'Well, I suppose you've talked to Jean', she sighed.

CORRECT: 'Well, I suppose you've talked to Jean,' she sighed.

Above all, avoid the comma splice: the joining-together of two independent statements incorrectly with the use of only a comma.

WRONG: It was a fine spring morning, Hamish decided to go for a walk by the shore.

CORRECT: It was a fine spring morning. Hamish decided to go for a walk by the shore.

It being a fine spring morning, Hamish decided to go for a walk by the shore.

Since it was a fine morning, Hamish decided to go for a walk by the shore.

A comma will not do the connection! Either use a full stop to acknowledge that these are two independent clauses or statements, or use connecting mechanisms such as the above. If in doubt, consult your teacher. A comma will not do the business here!

CHECK AGREEMENT

In longer sentences, where the subject may have become separated from the rest of the sentence – including the verb – make sure you have not started with a singular subject and ended up with a plural verb, or vice versa.

THINGS TO DO AND THINK ABOUT

Proofreading is the last stage in the long process of getting your portfolio together. You have put a great deal of work into these two pieces to get this far. You just cannot let yourself down by failing to spot typos, spelling errors, awkward expressions or ill-considered punctuation. These may have been spotted at an earlier stage but, with cutting and pasting, you may have let them slip back in. It can happen. Ensure that it doesn't!

GLOSSARY OF CRITICAL TERMS

At this stage of your studies, you need to be able to use the professional vocabulary of criticism to maximise the impact of your comments in spoken and written work. The following list is by no means comprehensive, but it gives you some of the more common terms to add to your critical vocabulary.

Alliteration
The repetition of a particular consonant – or consonant sound – at the beginning of a group of words to create a certain sound effect. *Cold clay clads his coffin.* Here the harsh sound of the letter 'c' matches the grimness of the description. *Soft sighing of the southern seas.* Here the soft 's' sound mimics the gentleness of the water's sound.

Anecdote
A brief story, often encountered in Close Reading passages, to illustrate a point.

Anti-climax
Often encountered when the final item in a list is the least important or oddly out of place. In Close Reading work, the effect is usually to add humour.

Assonance
The repetition of a certain group of similar-sounding vowels in words close to each other, again used to create a certain aural effect. *And murmuring of innumerable bees.* Assonance is to vowels what alliteration is to consonants.

Characterisation
The building-up and establishing of convincing character portrayals through means such as dialogue, actions or the reaction of others to the character in question.

Connotation
The associations we carry around in our minds – often unthinkingly – about certain words. For example, we associate 'dove' with peace, or 'rose' with love. Alternatively, verbs like 'cling' suggest an insecure, dependent frame of mind, while 'skip' suggests a light-hearted mood. Referring to connotations is often very useful for dealing with word choice or imagery questions in Close Reading.

Context
In Close Reading work, you may be asked to suggest how the context helps you to understand the meaning of a word. The context is the surrounding sentence or paragraph in which the word appears.

Denotation
Usually discussed in association with connotation. It is the dictionary definition of a word or term, free of the associations we have with connotations.

Ellipsis
In mid-sentence, these three dots can be used to suggest an interruption, hesitation or indecision. Used at the end of the sentence, they can suggest anticipation or suspense. *The door opened and a hand appeared …*

Enjambment
In poetry, this is the running-on of one line into another or into several others, either to give a conversational feel to the content or sometimes to suggest speeding-up for an effect of urgency. It can also make the reader wait for a key point to be made when the sentence finally stops.
… for my purpose holds
To sail beyond the sunset, and the baths
Of all the western stars, until I die.

Figurative language
This is language which uses figures of speech such as similes, metaphors or personification to create pictures ('figures') in our minds to make descriptions more vivid and graphic. It will often turn up in Close Reading work and literature study. Useful, too, in persuasive writing.

Foreshadow
Useful term for your critical essays or context work. A fairly minor event or incident can be said to 'foreshadow' a much more important one later in the text. It prepares the reader for a more significant event so that the later one is not wholly unexpected. For example, a mildly aggressive action can suggest a more violent one to come.

Genre
This is the type, or category, of literature: poetry, drama or prose. Genre also categorises the type of writing you may select for your Portfolio – discursive or creative being the main genres here.

Hyperbole
This is the technical literary name for exaggeration. It is often used to create a certain effect (often humorous) or to emphasise something. *The list goes on for miles. He never fails to get lost. I've seen more fat on a chip.* Hyperbole often turns up in tone questions in Close Reading. Can also be useful in persuasive writing.

Image/imagery
A device used to create a picture ('image') in the mind which exploits the connotations of a word to give it greater impact on the reader. Frequently at the core of questions in Close Reading work. Understanding of the working of imagery is also very necessary for commenting on literature and in your own creative writing where you wish to make a point with graphic vividness.

Irony
Often saying the opposite of what you mean. *The concert lasts four hours? With no interval? Wonderful!* Used frequently in questions of tone in Close Reading to criticise or mock something or somebody in a humorous or bitter way to make a critical point. Useful, too, in persuasive writing.

Literal/literally
Used when you want a word or phrase to mean exactly what it says, as opposed to being 'metaphorical' in its use, where the meaning is more figurative. For example, *My teacher went through the roof* is metaphorical, suggesting simply the anger of your teacher. If the phrase were used literally, it would suggest that your teacher did structural damage to the building.

Litotes
This is the opposite of hyperbole (see above), whereby something is understated rather than exaggerated, often for humorous effect. *Hamish is not the sharpest knife in the drawer* suggests that the intelligence of Hamish is somewhat limited.

Metaphor
This is a literary device whereby two items are compared. They are not, as in a simile, *like* each other; one *becomes* the other. *You're an angel. He was rocked by a tsunami of self-pity.*

Onomatopoeia
Here the sound of the word mimics and thereby gives a clue to its meaning. *Clink, fizz, rip, honk, boom, purr* are all words which suggest their meaning in their sound. *Bubbles gargled delicately* is an example of this used for aural effect by Seamus Heaney, suggesting a sound picture of the noise of bubbles emerging gently from mud at the bottom of a pond.

Oxymoron
The placing side by side of two words which appear to contradict each other, in order to startle and to create a vivid impact on the reader. *A deafening silence. A wise fool.*

Paradox
This is a form of extended oxymoron in which seemingly contradictory ideas are placed side by side. *The child is father of the man.* Its aim, like that of the oxymoron, is to arrest the reader's attention by its startling and, at first glance, puzzling nature.

Parallel structure
These are patterns of either phrases or words which give a pleasing predictability and rhythm to the sentence. The effect is to add emphasis to what is being said. *It is by logic we prove, but by intuition we discover* (da Vinci). *The ants were everywhere:* climbing *over jampots,* swarming *under the sink,* scrambling *into cupboards,* diving *into the bin.* The likeness of pattern here (preposition, noun, verb) makes for a more memorable phrase and creates a greater impact than a less patterned structure would.

Parenthesis
A parenthesis can be found between two dashes, two brackets or two commas. It is a phrase which adds interesting additional, but not essential, information to what is being discussed. It is often targeted by examiners in sentence-structure questions in Close Reading.

Personification
Personification is when an inanimate object is given living qualities. *The sun caressed her back. Hunger stalked the land.*

Repetition
This may take the form of repeated words or phrases to underline/intensify the idea the writer is seeking to emphasise at a particular point. *A good cyclist needs … A good cyclist hopes that … But a good cyclist knows above all that …* Note that these repetitions in the closing stages of a text might be building to a climax. Sentence-structure questions in Close Reading work may focus on this device.

Rhetorical question
These are questions expecting no direct answer, rather the reader's support for the writer's views. *Who wants to see a child suffer in this way?* Here the reader is expected to share the writer's horror at the ill-treatment of children.

Rhyme
The pairing of words with the same sound, used usually at the ends of lines in poetry:
On either side the river lie
Long fields of barley and of rye.
In more modern poetry, poets may attempt what is called a half-rhyme:
When have I last looked on
The round green eyes and the long wavering bodies
Of the dark leopards of the moon?
All the wild witches, those most noble ladies.
Here the words *on/moon* and *bodies/ladies* are related but not identical in sound, thus targeting aural cohesion but avoiding undue attention to rhyming words.

Rhythm
The pulse felt within a line of poetry, created through alternating unstressed and stressed syllables. *On either side the river lie …* or, alternatively, stressed and unstressed: *Willows whiten, aspens quiver.*

Sarcasm
Frequently expressed by uttering the opposite of what is meant. *My good friend, the traffic warden.* Be alert for this in tone questions in Close Reading work. You can also use it to good effect in your own persuasive writing.

Simile
One of the most common devices found in figurative language. It is a comparison between two items using 'like' or 'as': '*As idle as a painted ship upon a painted ocean*'. Used to bring the comparison vividly alive in the mind's eye.

Stanza
This is a means of referring to formal units in a poem, often when the units are of unequal length. For example, a Petrarchan sonnet has two stanzas: an octet followed by a sestet.

Style
This is a reference to how a writer creates effects in his or her work by, say, imagery, word choice, tone, anecdote, sentence structure or any other features which help to mark out the distinctive signature of that particular author or passage.

Symbolism
This is an item or action which stands for more than itself in a novel or poem. For example, a character might be seen to be pulling the petals off a flower, suggesting some later act of violence of a more serious nature.

Synonym
An alternative word for the same thing. Vital for success in understanding questions in Close Reading.

Theme
A central idea that binds together characters or situations in a novel or short story. It is what the text is *about.* For instance, the theme of the dangers of false appearance is everywhere you look in *Macbeth.* The Macbeths exploit it, as do the witches. Other people such as Duncan become its victim, as, ultimately, do the Macbeths themselves.

Tone
This is the unspoken attitude of writers to their subject. In Close Reading work, you are expected to tease this out by looking for internal clues such as hyperbole, emotive language or colloquial language.

Word choice
In RUAE work a question about this is one of the more common questions you will encounter. You need to select words from the text which appear to you to identify an effect or a tone that the writer is attempting to convey. For instance, does he/she refer to a woman as 'slim' or 'scrawny'? The word chosen will indicate his/her attitude to the woman in question, i.e. elegant and trim, or underweight to the point of being unattractive.